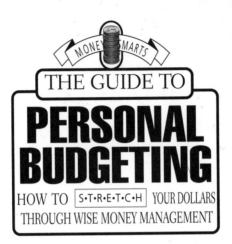

MONEY SMARTS

THE GUIDE TO

PERSONAL
BUDGETING

HOW TO S·T·R·E·T·C·H YOUR DOLLARS
THROUGH WISE MONEY MANAGEMENT

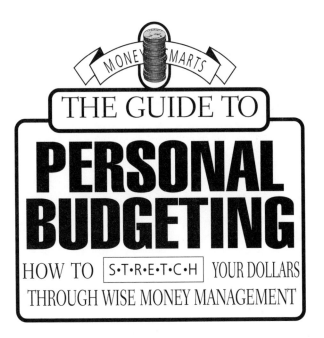

MONEY SMARTS

THE GUIDE TO

PERSONAL BUDGETING

HOW TO S·T·R·E·T·C·H YOUR DOLLARS
THROUGH WISE MONEY MANAGEMENT

All New Second Edition

by David L. Scott

The Globe Pequot Press

OLD SAYBROOK, CONNECTICUT

Library of Congress Cataloging-in-Publication Data

Scott, David Logan, 1942-
    The guide to personal budgeting : how to stretch your dollars through wise money management / by David L. Scott. — All new 2nd ed.
        p. cm. — (Money smarts series)
    Includes index.
    ISBN 1-56440-733-0
    1. Budgets, Personal—Handbooks, manuals, etc. I. Title. II. Series : Scott, David Logan, 1942- Money smarts.
HG179.S344   1995
640'.42—dc20   95-9314
                                                       CIP

Manufactured in the United States of America
Second Edition/First Printing

Contents

Introduction

If, at the end of each month, you wonder where your money went, this book is for you. *The Guide to Personal Budgeting* is written for people who would like to get a handle on their finances but don't know exactly how to go about it. You don't have to be versed in business or an expert in finance to establish and maintain a personal budget. Mostly, you need the proper amount of desire, a little common sense, and, perhaps, some guidance, which *The Guide to Personal Budgeting* provides. This book takes you on a step-by-step journey through the entire budgeting process—from the materials you will need and the information you should obtain before you begin, to how to enter and interpret the information on your budgeting forms. If you wish to use a personal computer, Chapter 6 explains how to set up budget worksheets using popular spreadsheet programs.

Sample budget forms are provided in figures throughout the book. Various kinds of forms can be used, so feel free to alter the samples. You can use a ruler to copy the forms onto blank sheets of paper, although it is more convenient to use ledger paper, which is available in office supply stores.

Be forewarned that a properly constructed personal budget can result in better money management but it cannot produce miracles. A budget can help you to make better decisions, to attain goals that might otherwise prove elusive, and to obtain more value for your money. A budget cannot cause money to appear mysteriously in your bank account, and a budget will not necessarily make it possible to put a Mercedes in your garage.

The bottom line is that maintaining a budget makes good sense. The budget will require time and effort, but the process and end product will put you in touch with your finances. A budget will help you decide what you can afford to buy and what you should pass over. Best of all, a budget, properly done, will help lead you to a brighter and more secure financial future.

CHAPTER 1

Why Budgeting Is Worthwhile

A personal budget can enable you and your family to gain control of your financial affairs. The budgeting process involves a review of your past income and spending, a listing and evaluation of your assets and outstanding loans, and a forecast of future income and expenses. Budgeting forces you to establish goals and make choices, two difficult tasks. A personal budget is valuable not only because it helps you to live within your means, but also because it prompts you to evaluate your entire financial situation.

A personal budget is a record-keeping system that will introduce organization and discipline to your financial affairs. Establishing and maintaining a budget can bring order to your financial affairs even if they are currently in a state of chaos. A budget is not a cure-all and cannot be expected to achieve the impossible, however. If you are currently earning $250 a week, it is unlikely that you will accumulate the funds necessary to acquire a new Mercedes no matter how diligently you work at maintaining a budget. Maintaining a personal budget requires effort, time, and persistence. Fortunately, successful budgeting does not require that you have extensive financial knowledge or that you are proficient with mathematics. As with many repetitive activities, the longer you maintain a personal budget, the more knowledgeable you will become and the easier the task will be. If you are willing to pay the modest price in time and effort, you will almost surely reap substantial rewards.

Individuals Most Likely to Benefit from a Budget

Individuals who complain that maintaining a budget is too difficult or time-consuming, or who rationalize that a budget will not produce any substantive improvement in their lives, are likely to be the very people who have the greatest need for the discipline a budget imposes. An unhappy truth is that many individuals avoid implementing a personal budget because they do not want to face the depressing numbers that a budget often presents. This situation is similar to that of people who are ill but avoid visiting the doctor because they don't want to hear the bad news. Also, people in financial difficulty may shy away from a personal budget because they are unwilling to curtail their habit of excessive spending.

A budget can produce significant benefits for the individual or the family that consistently encounters financial difficulties because of unwise spending decisions. People who are impressed with material possessions and who feel a need to be among the first to acquire new products (clothes, cars, electronic gadgets, and so forth) are likely to benefit from a budget.

Individuals who spend without considering cost are ideal candidates for a budget. A budget brings into play what economists call *opportunity cost:* The acquisition of one good or service means that you must forgo some other good or service; money spent for one thing is no longer available for something else. A budget brings opportunity cost into focus by requiring an individual to make choices.

Budgeting is a worthwhile endeavor if you cannot make ends meet, if you must scramble for funds at the end of each pay period, if you are unable to pay off the balances on your credit cards, and if you don't have the faintest idea of where your money goes each pay period. Budgeting is for you if you are unable to put money aside, if you have no idea how your kids will ever get through college (see Figure 1), and if you are concerned that you will never be able to afford to retire.

Try to repay your most expensive debt first. Your most expensive debt is likely to be the outstanding balances on your credit cards. It doesn't make much sense to prepay installments on a 9 percent mortgage when you have outstanding credit card debt that incurs an interest charge of 15 percent.

FIGURE 1

Estimated Annual Cost of Raising a Child Born in 1993

| Year | Age | Income Group | | |
		Lower	Middle	Highest
1993	<1	$4,960	$6,870	$10,210
1994	1	5,260	7,280	10,820
1995	2	5,570	7,720	11,470
1996	3	6,260	8,600	12,660
1997	4	6,640	9,120	13,420
1998	5	7,040	9,660	14,230
1999	6	7,830	10,580	15,250
2000	7	8,300	11,220	16,160
2001	8	8,800	11,890	17,130
2002	9	8,570	11,790	17,230
2003	10	9,080	12,500	18,270
2004	11	9,620	13,250	19,360
2005	12	11,070	14,870	21,490
2006	13	11,730	15,760	22,780
2007	14	12,430	16,710	24,150
2008	15	15,000	19,890	28,260
2009	16	15,900	21,080	29,950
2010	17	16,860	22,350	31,750
Total		**$170,920**	**$231,140**	**$334,590**

Source: Family Economics Research Group, Agricultural Research Service, U.S. Department of Agriculture, *Expenditures on a Child by Husband-Wife Families: 1993*

Individuals Who Are Unlikely to Benefit from a Budget

Tightfisted individuals may not realize substantial benefit from establishing and maintaining a personal budget. Fiscally conservative people are already likely to have a fairly accurate notion of how their funds are being spent, even without a written record of expenditures. Frugal individuals are often able to tuck away substantial amounts of money without the formal discipline imposed by a budget. The truth is, of course, that people who already closely monitor their spending habits are the very ones who are most likely to undertake a budget.

Another group for whom a budget may not be so important, at least not in the same manner as someone who is financially strapped, includes people who have such substantial income and assets that there is no need to scrutinize their spending. There are people in the world (although you may not personally know of any) who have so much money that they can purchase whatever they desire without straining their finances. The very wealthy frequently do not require the discipline imposed by a budget to keep their expenditures within their financial means because their financial means are so substantial.

Think about switching your long-distance phone company if you are offered a good deal. You may be offered a one-time bonus of $25 to $75 to change to a different carrier. You are likely to find that you can't distinguish the service of one provider from that of another.

Buy in quantity if the price is right. If a supermarket offers a real bargain on a cereal you like, buy several boxes. If you eat a lot of the cereal, buy a case. Do the same with soap, detergent, toilet paper, facial tissue, and so forth.

Despite an ability to satisfy their wants without financial strain, even wealthy individuals may secure benefits from maintaining a budget. The organization of financial affairs, which is inherent to the budgeting process, yields benefits that might be especially important for someone with a large income and substantial assets. Committing financial affairs to paper requires that you open your eyes to what you own, where it is located, and what it is worth. Thus, even wealthy individuals should reap some benefits from a budget, although the benefits may be somewhat different from those derived by persons with more modest levels of income and assets.

What a Budget Can Accomplish

1. *A budget can help you live within your financial means.* A budget requires that you maintain a written record of income and spending. Every week or month (depending on your chosen budgeting period), you must enter dollar amounts for the income you earn and the expenditures you make. The end product is a worksheet that brings financial imbalances into the open. A budget makes it obvious when spending is out of line with income, thus indicating that changes are necessary.

Income and spending are so closely intertwined that the linkage should be obvious; spending is constrained by the amount of income that is available. The truth is that relationships that are apparent on paper are not always so obvious in practice. Many individuals are either unable or unwilling to come to grips with the connection between income and spending so long as borrowing can be used to bridge any gap between the two. Only when creditors curtail further borrowing and an untenable life-style comes tumbling down do many people realize that an accounting must eventually take place.

2. *A budget can help you become a more intelligent consumer.* You are forced to become a wiser consumer when you must make choices among the goods and services you would like to acquire. Understanding that there is a limit to the things you will be able to acquire will cause you to give more consideration to choosing the goods and services that provide the greatest overall satisfaction. A major part of this consideration involves sifting through alternatives so that you obtain the greatest value per dollar spent. Realizing that careful shopping for groceries will make more funds available for a vacation or a new television produces more intelligent spending decisions. The disciplined system of spending effected by a budget contrasts with a more haphazard approach in which you purchase goods and services whenever the desire strikes, without being required to make choices.

When charging your purchases, use a credit card that offers an incentive. Several credit cards provide users with rebates that can be redeemed for free gasoline or discounts on computers or automobiles. The amount of the rebate depends on the amount you charge to your account. Why get nothing when you can get something for nothing?

3. *A budget can help you identify wasteful spending.* The spending record that is part of a personal budget can alert you to categories of products and services on which unusually large amounts of money are being spent. Many individuals remain in the dark about the amounts they spend for transportation, dining out, entertainment, and so forth. Although the cost of a particular item or service may be relatively small, repeated spending for that item or service during an entire budgeting period may add up to a substantial total. Examples of this kind of expenditure include eating out for lunch every day, drinking a few beers every night, and going to the movies every week. This is not to say that these activities cannot be included in a budget— they just have to be kept in perspective. Constructing a budget and examining the annual expenses for different categories of expenditures may cast the cost of a repeated small expenditure in a different light, especially if projections indicate that aggregate expenditures will exceed total income.

4. *A budget will allow you to attain important goals that might otherwise slip away.* Identifying and ranking financial goals form an important part of the budgeting process. Because most individuals and families normally cannot attain every identified goal, a ranking system will cause you to

Stay up-to-date on the rates local financial institutions are paying on various types of savings. You are likely to find that you can earn an extra ¼ to ½ percent by moving your savings to another institution. Don't let inertia and lack of knowledge cost you money.

> Use the telephone to comparison shop. There is no reason to spends lots of money driving from one store to the next looking for the lowest price. You may end up having to drive back to your first stop. Save both time and money by using your telephone.

concentrate on your primary goals or on the ones you are most likely to achieve. Thus, rather than spending funds on low-ranked goals or squandering most of your income on current consumption and doing nothing about achieving your goals, you pinpoint the goals and the costs of achieving them. At the same time, a budget motivates you to begin setting aside funds to attain your most important goals. Ranking the goals you establish is another example of how budgeting requires you to make choices.

5. *A budget can bring focus to your financial affairs.* Many individuals and families proceed through their entire lives without ever really coming to grips with their financial affairs. These people don't know exactly what they own, what they owe, or where they are headed. They probably have some thoughts about major goals they would like to achieve, but they have devoted no effort to determining how, when, or if the goals can be attained.

The budgeting process requires that specific information relative to your financial affairs be developed and recorded on paper. When you are required to think methodically about each of these topics—income, spending, goals, investing, and so forth—you can overcome a state of financial paralysis and begin to focus clearly on such matters. Budgeting is a good way to turn slipping and sliding from one paycheck to the next into an orderly march.

Comparing Personal Budgets
and Business Budgets

Nearly all successful businesses use the budgeting process as an important planning tool. Managers of a business need to know when money from sales and other sources of income will be received and when funds to pay employees and taxes and to purchase inventory and equipment will be required. Managers want to determine if cash payments to be received will be sufficient to take care of expected expenses and, if not, how the shortfall will be bridged. Successful managers do not wait until a cash crisis occurs before they seek outside sources of funding. These managers secure commitments for necessary financing before the funds are actually needed. Putting in place a system of financial planning not only makes it more likely that needed funds will be obtained, it may also result in acquiring the funds at a lower cost.

A personal budget is constructed in a somewhat different manner from a budget used by a business, although much of the information and many of the insights to be derived from a budget are similar for both an individual and the manager of a business. A personal budget provides an assessment of how your income (cash inflow) and spending (cash outflow) will compare in upcoming periods. The goal is to determine

Try not to run out of consumable items. Running out of a household staple means you will probably pay too much for a replacement because you don't have time to comparison shop or wait for a sale. If your stock of paper products starts to get low, begin looking for a sale.

Drive your vehicle a couple of years longer. Even though an older vehicle is likely to require increased maintenance expenses, the reduction in annual depreciation of an older vehicle makes extending the life of your current one a sure shot. The newer the vehicle you own, the greater your transportation expenses.

if forecasted spending will exceed income and, if so, what you intend to do about the projected deficit. If projected income exceeds projected expenditures, you will be required to determine how to deal with the surplus.

Timing differences

A budgeting problem encountered by nearly all businesses and some individuals stems from the occurrence of a large portion of income and expenses on an *accrued basis;* that is, a large portion of the sales that a business records as income does not result in any immediate cash payments. Rather, businesses often receive payments several weeks or even months after products or services have been delivered and the sale has been recorded as income. A steel company may sell and ship millions of dollars in products during a particular month but not receive payment for these sales for several months following shipment. Despite the delay in payment, the steel company will record the sale as income.

Accruals also occur on the opposite side of the transaction. Businesses frequently purchase goods and services with the understanding that payment is not due until some later date. Individuals do the same thing when purchases are made on credit. The delay between the date sales and expenses are recorded as income and the date payments for these sales and expenses actually occur requires that a business maintain a budget in which cash and noncash items are differentiated. Individuals are generally not subject to these same delays in income, although purchases may involve delayed payments when credit is used.

Now that you understand what a budget is designed to accomplish and why maintaining a budget is important, it is time to move forward and determine how to get started!

CHAPTER 2

Getting Started

The key to launching a budget is to sit down with paper and pencil (don't use a pen; you will need to erase) and begin. Drawing up a budget is not particularly difficult, but it helps to have certain items and information close at hand to make the process as easy as possible. The easier it is to maintain a budget, the less likely you are to find a reason to discontinue the budgeting process. This chapter provides many hints to help you over the initial hurdles of putting together a personal budget.

You will never know whether a personal budget can bring order to your financial affairs unless you give it a try, and you can't give it a try if paralysis keeps you from getting started. Often, substantial inertia keeps individuals from putting a budget in place. Many people, especially those who most need the discipline of a budget, never seem to find the time or energy to start. Set a date, begin the countdown, and prepare yourself. In the meantime try to build some enthusiasm for the undertaking among other family members.

An important component to beginning a budget successfully is to set aside adequate time to get organized. A little spadework in advance of the big event will facilitate the process. Advance work includes putting your hands on a few items that will be needed and obtaining certain kinds of information about your past income and spending. If you have a family, determine how best to get the other members involved in the planning and implementation of the budget. Perhaps most important, go into the process convinced that budgeting is a worthwhile endeavor and that you have the knowledge and resources to implement a budget successfully.

Consider using a discount brokerage firm to buy and sell securities. The fees at discount brokerage firms often run 50 to 80 percent lower than the fees charged by full-service brokerage firms. A number of discount brokerage firms advertise in most financial publications.

Bring the Correct Frame
of Mind to the Process

One key to success in maintaining a personal budget is to begin the process with the proper frame of mind. Start with the idea that a budget will introduce order to your financial affairs—an important change that will result in an improved quality of life for you and your family. There aren't many payoffs more important than this! The cost in time and effort to execute the budget in combination with the goods and services that may have to be sacrificed to meet the financial goals you have established are the price you must pay for an improved degree of financial security (and for some, perhaps, financial solvency).

Start with the attitude that executing a budget is not beyond your capabilities. There is nothing technically difficult about budgeting. The mathematics are simple; you merely need to be able to add and subtract. You may feel that you don't know how to estimate the dollar amounts that are required for a budget. Don't worry; in Chapter 5 you will discover that forecasting expenditures is not an impossible task, especially if you have the information listed later in this chapter.

The bottom line is that there is every reason to expect that you will be successful at initiating and maintaining a budget, even if you don't consider yourself to be particularly adept at business matters. You can handle a budget if you set your mind to it. The longer the budgeting process continues, the more proficient you will become and the less time you will spend working on your budget. In certain respects budgeting is like riding a bicycle; once you get started, the rest is a piece of cake.

Items You Will Need

A budget requires more in the way of willpower than it does physical items, but there are a few things that you will need to purchase if they are not already around the house. Here is a list of what you will need along with a short explanation for each item.

1. *A half dozen sharpened pencils.* Buy yourself some good pencils with lead that is soft enough so that you can clearly see your entries but not so soft that you end up with smudges across the budgeting sheets. Pencils with number 2 lead will work fine. Don't search through drawers for stubs of used pencils. You need to inject into the budgeting process some of the excitement that you felt when you were ready to start a new year of elementary school: new notebooks, new crayons (with pointed tips, no less), and new pencils. Pencils are better for making entries than pens because entries by pencil are easier to correct. Don't forget to have a few erasers ready!

2. *A ledger pad.* Begin the process with the correct forms for recording the required budgeting data. Visit a stationery store—or, even better, an office supply store—and browse through the many journals and ledger pads in stock. The

Ask if a particular product will soon be on sale before you purchase it. You may find that you can save a substantial amount of money by delaying your purchase of clothes, appliances, or furniture for another week or so.

> Pay your bills as late as possible without incurring a penalty. The later you pay your bills, the longer your funds are able to earn interest, an advantage for you. Insurance and credit card companies often send out bills weeks before payment is due. Why give up your money earlier than you have to?

main budget will require sheets that allow you to enter budgeting periods across the top (Week of Jan. 3, Week of Jan. 10, and so forth, or, alternatively, January, February, and so forth) and the dollar amounts of income and expenses directly below the appropriate budgeting periods.

You may want to use fairly large sheets for the summary budget statement in order to record on a single sheet as many budgeting periods as possible. The more information you can enter on a single sheet, the easier it is to make comparisons among the entries for different budgeting periods. Ledger sheets for a monthly budget should have at least twenty-six columns across the top (an alternative is to tape several sheets together): twelve columns for forecasted monthly income and forecasted monthly expenses, twelve columns for actual monthly income and actual monthly expenses, and two columns for annual summaries of both expected and actual income and expenses. You may decide to devote an additional monthly column to recording the differences between forecast income and expense items and actual income and expenditures. The extra column is useful for identifying spending categories in which you spend substantially more or less than planned.

Be certain the sheets have more than enough rows for all the income and expenditure categories you plan to include. As you gain experience with the budget, you may decide to

> Be realistic in the goals you establish. Setting unrealistic goals may cause you unnecessary depression when you find that you are unable to achieve your aims. You may also forgo attainable goals in a failed attempt to reach unattainable ones.

add new categories of both income and expenditures, so select forms that are sufficiently large to permit an expanded number of entries. Skim through Chapter 5 for a look at the types of forms you are likely to need.

3. *A small notebook for each family member.* Buy a notebook—small spiral notebooks work well—so each person involved in the budgeting process can maintain a record of all expenditures. Unless you have an unusually good memory, you are unlikely to remember every expenditure that is made during a day. You will need to record information for these expenditures while you are out there doing battle in the marketplace. Choose notebooks that are small enough to fit in your pocketbook or shirt pocket.

4. *Memo scratchpads.* If you categorize expenditures in your notebook (for example, one page for groceries, one page for transportation, one page for apparel, and so forth), there is no need for this purchase. If it is inconvenient to categorize expenditures in your notebook, consider purchasing a number of small scratchpads so that when you return home you can transfer information from your notebook to small sheets of paper. Choose the smallest size pads on which you can enter a few words and a dollar amount of spending. Also, choose the cheapest pads you can locate, because scratchpad sheets with entries will be discarded at the end of each budgeting period.

5. A small file folder designed for coupons or canceled checks. In transferring information from your notebook to scratch sheets, you will require a receptacle to hold the individual sheets. A small file folder with pockets labeled by spending category works fine. Most discount stores sell these folders in several sizes. An alternative is business envelopes to hold your spending notes. At the end of the month, transfer the totals from each envelope to your ledger, throw away the spending notes, and begin anew.

6. An easy-to-use calculator. If you don't already own a calculator, spend a few dollars and acquire one. You don't need a fancy model with a multitude of buttons. Settle for a cheap calculator that includes the four essential mathematical functions: addition, subtraction, multiplication, and division. No other functions matter. Budgeting will not require you to calculate the present value of a cash stream, determine the square root of a number, or determine the cosine of a function. Consider a solar model that has no batteries to replace. Select a model with keys that are large enough to accommodate your fingers (keys on some calculators are so small that you have to enter data with your fingernail or the end of a pencil). Purchase the calculator at a discount store such as Wal-Mart or Kmart, not the office supply store where you buy the ledger and notebooks. If you are going to start a personal budget, you may as well begin on the right foot and keep your expenses to a minimum.

> Try your best to make the budgeting process a family affair. Undertaking a budget without the assistance of other family members is almost surely a losing proposition.

Information You Will Need

You will need to look through your old paperwork and locate several pieces of information that will provide you with insight about some of the entries you will be making. Here is the short list of information sources you should have available when you begin your budget.

1. *A recent paycheck stub.* A paycheck stub serves as a good source of information for income and certain expense items. Each week's (or month's) check stub contains data about your gross pay, social security contribution, federal income tax withholding, state income tax withholding, and, most important, your take-home pay (the amount of the check). The final paycheck of the prior year is particularly useful because it often contains all of this information for both the entire year and the last pay period of the year.

2. *Last year's federal income tax return.* Last year's federal tax return is a good source of budgeting information. In particular locate Form 1040 (the front and main form of the return), Schedule A (the schedule of itemized deductions), and Schedule B (the listing of interest and dividends that were received during the year). You may or may not have used Schedule A or Schedule B on last year's return. If your return did not include one or both of these schedules, don't worry, the budgeting process will be just that much easier.

> It is dangerous to choose long-term investments to meet short-term goals. Long-term investments generally have volatile values, high fees, and can be expensive to liquidate. Use short-term investments to meet short-term goals.

Include an inflation factor when you estimate the cost of long-term goals. The cost of most long-term goals is likely to be substantially higher than the current cost of these same goals. Even a nominal inflation rate can have a significant effect on the price of something over many years.

3. Checkbook registers containing your past year's checking activity. Entries in your checkbook register should refresh your memory relative to expenditures you made during the past year. The register's usefulness depends on how frequently you write checks and how diligently you record the information. (Some lazy people record only the dollar amount of each check, not the payees—a terrible practice.) If you are the type of person who writes checks for virtually every purchase, the checkbook register will be a treasure trove of information for your budget. Here, in a single source, you have a detailed record of an entire year's expenditures. If you typically write checks for cash and then make expenditures in cash, or use a credit card and mostly write checks to pay credit card bills, the checkbook register will be of little value. Keep it at hand, anyway.

4. Monthly credit card statements for the last year. Credit card statements are a valuable source of spending information for the same reason that checkbook registers prove useful: The statements contain data to indicate how you have been spending money. The more you rely on credit cards to pay for goods and services, the more valuable credit card statements will be for forecasting your expenditures. If you have been trashing each statement after checking its accuracy, you should have your hand slapped.

Breaking the News to Family Members

Your fling at establishing a personal budget is certain to fail unless you involve everyone who is to be affected by the budget. Each person who contributes to or spends from the family's common pool of money must become involved in the budget. Budgeting units may include a husband, wife, children, plus any additional dependents who live in the same home. Exclude individuals who live with you but who operate as independent income and spending units (you may sometimes feel that other family members all operate independently even though you supply the monetary resources). For example, a son or daughter with full-time employment may temporarily continue to live in your house. If this family member does not spend from or contribute to a common family pool of money, he or she should not be included in your budget.

Family members who are not involved in establishing the budget will have no stake in the budget's success. Without input into the process, these members are more likely to continue spending in the same manner as before the budget was initiated. Also, without the assistance of other family members, you will find it difficult to maintain an accurate record of income and spending.

Before initiating a budget, call together all the family members (use a platter of snacks as bait). Discuss what the

Using the net amount of your paycheck rather than gross pay simplifies the budgeting process because you don't have to account for taxes and other items that are withheld from your pay by your employer.

budget is designed to accomplish and why you feel the family will be better off with a budget. Mention the benefits of maintaining a budget, but don't spare the downside: the work that will be involved, along with some reigning in of spending that may be required. The chances are that you are considering a budget because you have already encountered financial difficulties. Without blaming any particular person, bring these problems into the open so that everyone will understand why changes in the management of your finances are required.

An established set of financial goals is a key element of a budget. Goal setting is a crucial task in which all family members must participate—a fact that should be stressed to the participants. Establishing and ranking goals should be a collective process in order to convince family members that they each have a stake in making the budgeting process a success. If family members can be convinced that maintaining a budget will make it more likely that the family will obtain things that are really desired, the individual members are more likely to work with you rather than against you. The process of establishing and achieving goals is addressed in Chapter 3.

It may be helpful to have younger family members treat the budgeting process as a game. Offer rewards to individual members who successfully maintain a record of spending or who remind other family members to record expenditures. Establish a system of rewards for the entire family when goals are attained. Make the budgeting process a family activity as opposed to a grueling ordeal that family members regard as punishment.

As part of the introduction, make family members aware of the forms that will be used in the budgeting process.

There is no need to overwhelm everyone with these forms. In the first get-together it may be best to merely pass them around and briefly discuss each one.

At the completion of each budgeting period, when all income and spending transactions have been sorted and entered onto the proper forms, and after the spending categories have been summarized, call another family meeting to examine the results. Were you able to keep expenditures within the established limits? Which categories of spending were closest to being on target, and which categories were furthest from your forecasts? Should you refine subsequent estimates for certain categories of spending? Does it appear that some of the goals you established should be sacrificed so that other goals can be attained? These are all important issues that should be examined jointly.

CHAPTER 3

Establishing and Attaining Financial Goals

Establishing goals is an important part of the budgeting process. Goal setting involves identifying goals, determining the cost of each identified goal, deciding when individual goals are to be achieved, and calculating how much money must be set aside each budgeting period to attain the identified goals. Most individuals and families cannot attain every desired goal, so decisions must be made as to which goals are most important. This chapter discusses how to establish goals and how to determine the amounts of money to put aside each period to achieve the identified goals.

Perhaps you have been thinking that you would like to retire at a relatively young age so that you and your spouse will have time to enjoy a few of the things the two of you have spent years dreaming about. How much money will be required, and how much income should you be setting aside each month to attain the goal of an early retirement? Or maybe you are tired of living in an apartment and would like to purchase your own home. What size down payment will be required, and how much will you have to stash away each month to accumulate this amount? To complicate the problem, how are your calculations affected if you anticipate that inflation will increase the eventual cost of attaining these goals?

If you haven't already come to grips with these kinds of questions, the start of the budgeting process is a good time to begin. The process is simple: Identify your goals, rank them in order of importance, estimate the cost of attaining each goal, establish approximate dates for attaining each goal, and determine the amount of money that must be set aside each budgeting period to attain your goals.

Identifying Goals

The first order of business is to identify the goals that are appropriate for you and your family. Begin the process by asking each family member to identify from three to six

Don't forget to budget for the taxes you will be required to pay on investment income. Unless your employer withholds too much from your paycheck, you will have to come up with the taxes for the investment income you earn.

goals that he or she considers to be important. Some financial advisers suggest that you divide the goals into three classifications: long-term (more than five years), intermediate-term (one to five years), and short-term (less than one year). Here are some sample goals.

Long-term goals
  comfortable retirement
  college education for the children
  vacation home

Intermediate-term goals
  emergency fund
  "see-the-USA" vacation
  down payment on a home
  new automobile
  swimming pool
  remodeled kitchen
  new roof

Short-term goals
  summer vacation
  new washer and dryer
  automobile insurance premium
  homeowner's insurance premium
  life insurance premium
  summer camp for the children

Allow several days before meeting again as a group to sort through the ideas. You might request that each goal be written on a separate piece of paper so that recommendations can be discussed one at a time without identifying who originated each suggestion. Separate pieces of paper

So-called flexible-spending benefit plans for medical expenses and child care can produce substantial tax savings. If you choose to enroll in such a plan, begin with a conservative estimate for upcoming expenses since any amounts that have been withheld by your employer cannot be recovered except for expenditures you incur.

may also prove to be handy for sorting goals by priority and category. Depending on family size and the ages of family members, you may find that some goals are unrealistic and other goals are of limited interest to all but one person. Still, it is important that each suggestion receive a fair hearing. Bringing individuals into the decision-making process will make them more willing participants in the budgeting process.

Determining the Cost of a Goal

Estimated cost should be an important determinant in awarding a priority to a particular goal—the greater the cost of a particular goal, the greater the number of alternative goals that must be sacrificed to attain it. Some goals may be so costly that it is unreasonable to assume they can ever be attained.

The current costs of most goals—a fully funded college fund, a particular automobile, a house—are fairly easy to determine. Merely call the appropriate business—college admissions office, car dealer, real estate agent—and ask about the price. The costs of other goals, such as an adequate retirement fund or an adequate emergency fund, are more difficult to determine.

After estimating the costs of individual goals, determine the dates by which you wish to attain each goal. The dates to meet short-term goals are relatively easy to estimate. Certain goals, such as insurance premium payments, have predetermined dates, whereas other goals allow more flexibility. Is it your intention to trade cars next year, in two years, or in three years? If you are now driving a clunker, acquiring the funds to buy a car may be a short-term goal. If you normally trade cars only because you have a preference for driving a newer car (you trade because you want to, not because you have to), there will be flexibility in setting the date to trade.

The longer the time before you plan to attain a particular goal, the less money you need to save each period in order to accumulate the funds necessary to achieve that goal. For example, if you plan to trade automobiles in two years rather than three years, you must set aside more money each month.

Adjusting for Inflation

Inflation is not normally much of a problem when you estimate the costs of short-term goals. Unless inflation is severe, goals targeted for a year or two in the future won't end up costing much more than the amount of your current estimate. Thus, meeting many short-term goals requires only that you accumulate the funds that would be necessary to make the same purchases today while assuming that the cost of a goal will remain the same.

A major difficulty when working with intermediate-term and long-term goals is that costs often prove to be moving

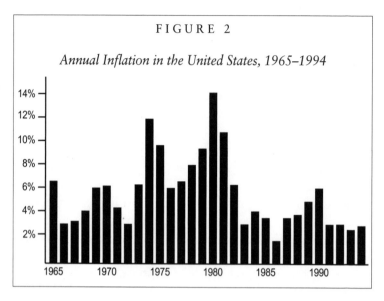

FIGURE 2

Annual Inflation in the United States, 1965–1994

targets. Someone who is saving in order to accumulate a down payment on a home may discover that housing values increase each year, thereby causing the required down payment to increase. Likewise, your family may decide to put aside funds to pay for a major vacation that is to be taken in three years only to realize that increases in travel costs between the time the goal is set and the time the travel takes place make the original cost estimate inadequate. As a result, your savings are not sufficient to pay for the planned vacation, and your family may have to settle for a two-week trip to Boise, Idaho, rather than a three-week vacation in San Francisco.

Estimating the eventual cost of attaining a long-term goal presents a problem because even modest inflation rates can have a substantial effect on the cost of a good or service over a long period. For example, a relatively modest but persistent annual inflation rate of 5 percent will increase the cost of a good or service by more than two and a half times over a twenty-year period. Likewise, goods and services will double in cost in only ten years if prices increase at an annual rate of 7 percent.

Several methods can be employed to account for an expected increase in the cost of a goal. One method is to adjust the goal's current cost for the inflation that is expected to occur between the time the goal is identified and the time it is to be attained. Suppose you have set a goal to purchase a new car in four years, and you do not want to have to borrow any money to finance the purchase (that is, you want to save enough to pay cash). The car you are interested in purchasing could be bought today for $14,000. You realize that it is unlikely the price of the car will remain the same, which means you will need to have accumulated savings of more than $14,000 at the time you intend to make the purchase. The problem is to determine the amount of money required in four years to pay for the new vehicle.

Figure 3 provides numerical factors that can be used to calculate the future worth of a sum of money and to figure out how much something is likely to cost on a future date given the cost today. To determine the future cost of a good or service, multiply its current cost by the table factor that is appropriate for the inflation rate and the length of time that applies to the item in which you are interested. Suppose you

> Save over time in order to pay cash for a major purchase rather than borrow the funds and pay the creditor over time. The first choice is much cheaper than the second.

FIGURE 3

Factors for Calculating Future Dollar Amounts

Annual Rate of Increase

No. of Years	2%	3%	4%	5%	6%	7%	8%	9%
1	1.020	1.030	1.040	1.050	1.060	1.070	1.080	1.090
2	1.040	1.061	1.082	1.102	1.124	1.145	1.166	1.189
3	1.060	1.093	1.093	1.125	1.191	1.225	1.260	1.295
4	1.082	1.126	1.170	1.216	1.263	1.311	1.361	1.412
5	1.104	1.159	1.217	1.276	1.338	1.403	1.469	1.539
6	1.126	1.194	1.265	1.340	1.418	1.501	1.587	1.677
7	1.149	1.230	1.316	1.407	1.504	1.606	1.714	1.828
8	1.172	1.267	1.369	1.478	1.594	1.718	1.851	1.993
9	1.195	1.305	1.423	1.551	1.690	1.838	1.999	2.172
10	1.219	1.344	1.480	1.629	1.791	1.967	2.159	2.367
15	1.346	1.558	1.801	2.079	2.397	2.759	3.172	3.642
20	1.486	1.806	2.191	2.653	3.207	3.870	4.661	5.604
25	1.641	2.094	2.666	3.386	4.292	5.427	6.848	8.623
30	1.812	2.427	3.243	4.322	5.744	7.612	10.060	13.270

think the car of your dreams is likely to increase in price by about 5 percent annually during each of the next four years. To determine the cost of the car at the time you plan to make the purchase, multiply the current cost of the car ($14,000) by the table factor at four years in the 5 percent column. In this instance the car should have a selling price of approximately $14,000 times 1.216, or $17,024, at the time you plan to make your purchase in four years.

How do you determine the appropriate rate of inflation to apply to a particular goal? One way is to observe current and past inflation rates and make some assumption as to the rate of inflation that will occur during the period you are setting funds aside. Another method is to read the financial pages of a newspaper or news magazine and determine the inflation rate that "experts" are forecasting. Remember that measures of inflation such as the Consumer Price Index maintained by the U.S. Department of Labor are based on a great variety of goods and services and can differ from the price changes of an individual good or service. If you don't have any luck at either of these methods of determining an inflation estimate, call the economics department at a local college and ask someone who studies this subject.

The factors in Figure 3 have uses other than calculating the effects of inflation. Suppose you plan to invest $5,000 in a five-year certificate of deposit that pays a 7 percent annual return. At the time you purchase the certificate, you request that interest income be automatically reinvested rather than paid to you each period. To determine the amount of money you will receive when the certificate matures, multiply the $5,000 original amount you invested by the table factor at the appropriate interest rate (7 percent) for the appropriate time (five years). The certificate will amount to $5,000 times 1.403, or $7,015, at maturity.

Purchase items on the basis of unit cost, not total cost. The larger size is not always the best bargain. Take a small calculator with you when you go shopping.

Determining How Much to Set Aside Each Period

Once you have estimated a goal's eventual cost, the next step is to calculate the amount of money that must be set aside each period to attain that goal. It is not necessary to use separate accounts or investments to set aside the funds that will be used to meet different goals (although you may want to maintain separate records for your own use). In other words, you do not need to establish one savings fund for trading cars, a separate fund for taking a vacation to Seward, Alaska (not a bad place to visit in the summer), and yet another fund to pay for a major remodeling of your kitchen. It is more convenient and practical to keep all your funds in a limited number of investments.

Determining the amount that must be set aside each period to meet short-term goals is a relatively easy task. First, the time interval to attain short-term goals is generally so limited that inflation and interest to be earned on money you have set aside are not particularly important because the current cost of the item to be acquired is not likely to change much. With no need to adjust for inflation, you can determine the monthly or weekly amounts to be set aside by dividing the number of budgeting periods until the goal is to be met into the cost of the goal. For example, suppose your family has decided that an important goal is to take a vaca-

> The less discipline you have as a consumer, the more you can benefit from avoiding credit purchases. If you always purchase for cash, you are much less likely to get into financial difficulty than if you purchase on credit.

tion next summer, and you estimate the cost of the trip at $3,000 (traveling is expensive). The monthly amount that must be set aside is equal to the $3,000 estimated cost divided by twelve periods (if the vacation is to be taken in twelve months), or $250. If you maintain a weekly budget, you will need to set aside $3,000 divided by 52, or about $58 per week. If you are planning to take the vacation in two years, you will need to set aside about $125 each month, or $29 each week. It is best to round the numbers up to the nearest whole dollar.

Periodic Saving to Meet Long-term Goals

Determining the amount to set aside each period to meet long-term goals is somewhat complicated for two reasons. First, the cost of meeting a long-term goal is often difficult to determine. Second, you must account for the interest income that your funds will earn during the years between when the savings are set aside and when the money is needed. Interest earned by your savings can amount to a substantial portion of the required funds if many years elapse before the funds will be needed. The higher the return you earn on your savings, the less money you must set aside each period in order to accumulate a certain amount of savings.

Suppose that you are attempting to determine how much to put aside each year in order to pay for your three-year-old son's college education. (You reckon that if he can make good grades in undergraduate school, perhaps he will go on to medical school, become a medical specialist, and feel a sense of obligation to support you following your early retirement.) The boy will start his first year of college in fifteen years, and you estimate that tuition and living expenses will require that you have approximately $40,000 available at the start of the first year of school. Inflation has already been factored into this cost estimate.

The method used to calculate the savings requirement for attaining a short-term goal, dividing $40,000 by fifteen years (the number of years before the funds will be needed), is inadequate to calculate the savings requirement to meet this long-term goal because it includes no adjustment for investment income that your funds will earn during the fifteen years. The bottom line is that you will be able to meet your target by putting aside less than $2,667 ($40,000 divided by fifteen years) annually, but how much less?

The factors in Figure 4 can be used to calculate the annual amount of savings required to accumulate a specific sum of money in a certain number of years at an assumed rate of return. To calculate the amount that needs to be saved each year, divide the amount to be accumulated by the table factor that is appropriate for the rate of return and the number of years you are assuming. For example, the annual savings to accumulate $5,000 in five years, when your funds will earn an average of 6 percent annually, is calculated as $5,000 divided by 5.637 (the table factor for five years and 6 percent), or $887. In this case you put aside a total of $4,435 (five payments of $887 each), and the remaining $565 is derived from investment income that is earned by your funds. The factors in Figure 4 assume that saving occurs at the end, not the beginning, of each period.

To determine the amount you must annually set aside to accumulate your son's college fund, you must first estimate the annual rate of return your funds will earn over the fif-

FIGURE 4

Factors for Calculating Periodic Saving to Meet Goals

Annual Return on Savings

Year	2%	3%	4%	5%	6%	7%	8%	9%
1	1.000	1.000	1.000	1.000	1.000	1.000	1.000	1.000
2	2.020	2.030	2.040	2.050	2.060	2.070	2.080	2.090
3	3.060	3.091	3.122	3.152	3.184	3.215	3.246	3.278
4	4.122	4.184	4.246	4.310	4.375	4.440	4.506	4.573
5	5.204	5.309	5.416	5.526	5.637	5.751	5.867	5.985
6	6.308	6.468	6.633	6.802	6.975	7.153	7.336	7.523
7	7.434	7.662	7.898	8.142	8.394	8.654	8.923	9.200
8	8.583	8.892	9.214	9.549	9.898	10.260	10.640	11.030
9	9.755	10.160	10.580	11.030	11.490	11.980	12.490	13.020
10	10.950	11.460	12.010	12.580	13.180	13.820	14.490	15.190
15	17.290	18.600	20.020	21.580	23.280	25.130	27.150	29.360
20	24.300	26.870	29.780	33.070	36.790	41.000	45.760	51.160
25	32.030	36.460	41.650	47.730	54.860	63.250	73.110	84.700
30	40.590	47.580	56.080	66.440	79.060	94.460	113.300	136.300

teen years you will be saving to meet this goal. Suppose you use a conservative estimate that your funds will earn an annual return of 5 percent. To accumulate $40,000 in fifteen years, you will need to set aside $40,000 divided by the table factor 21.58, or $1,854, each year. If you assume a higher return—say, 6 percent annually—you will need to set aside only $1,718 each year.

The difference between the total amount of money you will be setting aside—$1,854 times fifteen, or $27,810—and the $40,000 amount that will be available in fifteen years demonstrates the importance of investment income in meeting a savings goal when a long period of time is involved. In this instance your funds will earn more than $12,000, or 30 percent of the total that is needed. The difference between the required payment when a return of 5 percent is assumed and the required payment when a return of 6 percent is assumed illustrates the importance of the size of the return to the amount that you must set aside each period. The higher the return your investment earns, the more that investment income contributes to meeting a goal and the less money you must put aside each period to accumulate a specific sum of money.

Figure 5 illustrates the importance of investment income to meet your long-term goal of accumulating a college fund. Each bar in the figure represents the total amount of funds that will be in the fund in a particular year. The bottom section of each bar is the total amount of money you have put aside, and the top portion of each bar represents the total amount of investment income your funds will have earned up until that point. The sum of these two amounts is the total amount of money in your college fund.

If you maintain a monthly budget and wish to convert the required savings into a monthly amount, merely divide the annual amount to be saved by twelve. In the case of the college fund earning a 5 percent return, monthly savings of

Don't throw away old check registers and credit card statements. Both are excellent sources of spending information that can be used when you go about putting together your budget. They can also serve as reference sources when you want to determine how much you paid for something.

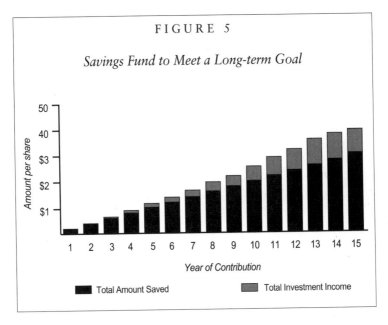

FIGURE 5

Savings Fund to Meet a Long-term Goal

Year of Contribution

■ Total Amount Saved   ▨ Total Investment Income

$155 ($1,854 divided by twelve) will be required. If you maintain a weekly budget, divide the annual amount to be saved by fifty-two. Although investment income earned by monthly or weekly savings deposits will differ somewhat from the interest that will be earned from annual deposits, the difference is not sufficiently important to justify adding another complication to the calculation.

Now let's try another example to test your skill at determining the amount of money that must be periodically set aside to accumulate a certain amount of money. Suppose a contractor has estimated a current cost of $18,000 to build an additional room on your home. You hope to undertake the addition in seven years and expect inflation to add 5 percent annually to construction costs. To pay for the addition, you will set aside a fixed amount each month. You expect to be able to earn an annual return of 7 percent on your invested funds. First, use Figure 3 to determine how much the addition will cost in seven years. Second, use Figure 4 to calculate the annual amount you must save in order to accumulate the inflation-adjusted cost of the room. The correct answer is $2,927 divided by twelve, or $244 per month.

After Your Calculations Are Complete

After your goals have been identified and you have determined when the goals are to be attained, estimated the costs of the goals, and calculated the periodic amounts that must be saved to accumulate the required funds, you are ready for a really tough challenge—setting priorities among the identified goals. If, like most people, you will be unable to attain all of your identified goals, you now have valuable information to help you rank proposals on the basis of cost as well as on the basis of how strongly you desire to attain each goal. Figure 6 illustrates how you may want to set out the information on goals.

All family members who have been involved in establishing goals should be involved in sorting through them once the costs have been estimated. The real cost of acquiring something—forgoing other goods and services— becomes apparent when family members realize that attaining a particular goal may require the family to save substantial sums of money over many periods. This saving can be achieved only by sacrificing current consumption or by forgoing other goals.

FIGURE 6

Goal Worksheet

Goal	Amount Needed	Date Needed	Number of Months to Save	Date to Start Saving	Periodic Amount to Save
Washer and dryer	$800	June '96	8	Nov. '95	$100
Automobile	17,000	Dec. '99	60	Jan. '95	250
Vacation	950	July '96	19	Jan. '95	50
General savings	N/A	N/A	N/A	Jan. '96	50
Emergency fund	5,300	Dec. '98	48	Jan. '95	100

One goal that should receive a high priority is the establishment of an adequate emergency fund. Every person and family should have funds set aside in case a problem such as illness, unemployment, injury, or loss of a personal asset occurs (for instance, you crash your car). An emergency fund is a financial resource that you can tap for money when a financial problem develops. Many financial planners recommend that families maintain an emergency fund equal to six months' after-tax income.

Goals that require substantial savings requirements may cause you to postpone the target dates in order to reduce the weekly or monthly saving requirement. Rather than planning to trade cars in two years, you may decide to stretch the target date to three years. The additional year will allow for reduced monthly saving to attain the goal at the same time that it will free funds for other needs. There is nothing demeaning about postponing the target date for achieving one or more goals you have set. In fact, one purpose of developing a budget is to provide guidance on what is possible and what is not possible.

The ability to attain goals is affected not only by the amount of income you take home, but also by the amounts that you must spend on other goods and services—such things as food, rent, utilities, and insurance premiums. There are many needs that must be taken care of before you can begin setting aside funds for attaining long-term goals.

The necessity to satisfy current needs doesn't mean that long-term goals can be funded only from the money that remains after you have taken care of all your other expenses. You have a degree of control over the amount of money that is spent on many of your current needs. In other words, accumulating funds for a summer vacation—one of your identified goals—may require that you reduce spending on food or on some other immediate needs. For instance, you decide to adjust the thermostat in your home to save on utilities in order to free funds for other purposes. Most families are able to reduce some of their current expenditures if the goal is sufficiently important and the willpower is present. Everything is a trade-off. Whenever you spend money on one thing, you are giving up something else. Maintaining a personal budget should make clear that this trade-off exists so that you are able to view the real cost of attaining a goal.

The important points discussed in this chapter—identifying, ranking, and determining the costs of goals—are a prelude to Chapter 5, which discusses how to build the outlays for attaining these goals into your main budget.

CHAPTER 4

The Balance Sheet: What You Own and Owe

Every individual and family should maintain a current accounting of what is owned and what is owed. Up-to-date and accurate information about your *assets* (things of value you own) and *liabilities* (amounts you owe) is important in making decisions relative to buying insurance, writing a will, and establishing goals. This chapter discusses how to take an inventory of what you own, how to determine what you owe, and how to incorporate this information into a financial statement that accountants call a *balance sheet*.

Unfortunately, many individuals have no clear idea of what they own and how much these things are worth. Family members know that they own a house, two cars, clothes to fill six closets, a washer and dryer, three television sets, and so forth. It is less likely that these people can list all their possessions along with even a close approximation of the dollar amount that each is worth. For example, how much money is currently in your savings account? How much is your household furniture worth? How much would your retirement fund be worth if you quit work or were laid off? How about your life insurance policies? Your automobiles?

Just as a personal budget requires that you come to grips with how your income is spent, a balance sheet requires that you determine the values of the things that you own and how much you owe to creditors. Any individual who is attempting to get a handle on his or her financial affairs must have knowledge of the values of things that are already owned and how much is owed.

How Businesses Put Together a Balance Sheet

A balance sheet that lists assets and liabilities is one of the two primary financial statements that are used by a business. The other major financial statement, an *income statement,* is a record of income and expenses for a particular time period and is similar to the personal financial statement discussed in the next chapter. Managers of businesses construct financial statements to assist them in determining how effectively the firms are being operated, to allow owners to judge the firms' profitability, and to show lenders how creditworthy the firms are. A manager operating a business without a current income statement and balance sheet is similiar to a driver taking a cross-country trip without a speedometer or odometer.

A business's balance sheet lists everything of value that the firm owns as well as all the firm's outstanding loans. The difference between the value of what the firm owns and the amount the firm owes represents the current value of what the owners have invested in the firm, either through the purchase of stock from the firm or from the firm's reinvestment of profits.

Businesses generally list assets according to how easily they can be converted into cash. Assets that are easily exchanged for cash—short-term securities, inventories, and customer accounts that will soon be paid—are listed first. These easily convertible assets are called *current assets*. Assets other than current assets include investments in other companies, equipment, buildings, and land.

Money owed by the firm is listed in a separate category called *liabilities*. Liabilities are listed in order of how soon the loans must be repaid. Loans that must be paid soon—loans from suppliers, short-term bank loans—are listed first, and loans that have long payoffs—loans to purchase equipment or a building—are entered last. The loan amount listed

Save money by purchasing checks from a source other than your local financial institution. Outside printing companies often sell checks for 40 to 50 percent of what you pay to purchase checks from your bank, credit union, or savings and loan. Advertisements by these firms can be located in a variety of publications, including the supplements to many Sunday newspapers.

> Don't get discouraged in the early going if spending in various categories of your personal budget is substantially different from your forecasts for these categories. Improvement of your estimates is a continuing process and the accuracy of your forecasts will increase over time. Major discrepancies call attention to categories of spending that may have been a major cause of financial difficulties.

on the balance sheet is the outstanding balance—the original amount that was borrowed less any payments of principal (not including interest) that have been made. The outstanding balances for most long-term loans decline over time as the firm makes payments to the lenders.

The dollar difference between the value of assets the firm owns and the outstanding loan balances is termed *net worth*, or stockholders' *equity*. Net worth is the current dollar investment that owners have in the business. Ideally, the business will grow in terms of sales and profits so that the net worth of owners will increase over time. An increase in net worth is one mark of a successful company.

Your Personal Balance Sheet Is Similar to the Balance Sheet of a Business

A personal balance sheet is constructed in almost the same manner as the balance sheet of a business. You list the things that you own in terms of how easily these items can be sold. You then determine the amounts you owe on your credit cards, car loans, mortgage, and any other outstanding debts. The total of the outstanding balances on the loans represents the amount of assets that are financed with borrowing. If the values of your assets and outstanding loans are equal, everything that you own is financed with borrowed money. The extent to which the value of your assets exceeds the outstanding balances on your loans represents assets that you own free and clear of debt. Essentially, your net worth measures the dollar value of what you have been able to accumulate over your lifetime. Ideally, your net worth is positive and is increasing each budgeting period.

Like a business balance sheet, your personal balance sheet shows what is owned and owed at a particular time. There is no specific time that is necessarily best to construct a personal balance sheet, although many individuals may find the end of the calendar year to be convenient for determining the values for many balance sheet entries. Many financial institutions send reports listing income, assets, and loan balances as of December 31, and financial publications sometimes offer special editions with end-of-year security values. This doesn't mean that you should wait until the end of the year to get started, however. You should begin as soon as possible and then follow up with a revised year-end balance sheet.

Businesses usually recalculate their balance sheets every three months because they are required to provide owners with a quarterly accounting of income, assets, and liabilities. Maintaining a quarterly balance sheet involves a lot of work, so you may decide to compute this financial statement once each year. An annual updating of assets and liabilities generally works fine for individuals.

Try to maintain accurate and complete records of spending and income. Lack of organization often explains a large part of a family's financial difficulties.

Although a personal balance sheet and a business balance sheet are similar, the two statements are not identical. When making out your personal balance sheet, you should value your assets at their current market values. If you own a home, you should enter its current market value on your personal balance sheet; likewise, you should use the current market value of your car, even though the car will have a market value less than the price you paid and different from the balance on the loan to finance the car. Both the home and auto values are entered without regard to any loans that were made to acquire the assets or that remain outstanding at the time the valuation takes place. Borrowings are entered separately on the balance sheet.

Many personal assets—a car, for example—decrease in value over time, so most of the assets you list are likely to have current values that are less than the purchase prices. Other assets—your home, perhaps, and most of the investments you own—may have increased in value since they were acquired. Only the current value of an asset is considered when a personal balance sheet is constructed. The original cost of the asset is of no consequence when you enter the asset on your balance sheet.

A personal balance sheet does not include separate entries for the funds that have been set aside to meet each of your goals. Balance sheet assets such as savings accounts, certificates of deposit, stocks, and so forth include the funds you have been setting aside to attain your established goals. List-

Controlling spending requires the same type of self-discipline as controlling calorie intake. Control must become a continuing process to be successful.

ing the current market values for all your investments and also including the amounts you have accumulated to meet each goal is double counting. The funds that will be used to attain your goals do not sit in separate investment pools; they are included as part of the portfolio of investments you own.

Both businesses and individuals value liabilities in an identical manner; that is, a liability is entered as the dollar amount of the remaining balance on the loan. If you borrowed $80,000 when you purchased your home ten years ago and a balance of $62,000 remains on the loan, use $62,000 as the entry for this liability. The original amount of the loan is not relevant for the balance sheet entry.

Collecting Information About Your Assets

The first order of business is to develop a list of the things that you own. There is no way that you will remember to list everything you own, of course, but be comforted by the thought that most of the things that you will forget are relatively unimportant. The major items are the ones that you do not want to leave out. You should list each of the valuable things that you own: a home, cars, securities, jewelry, and whatever other items of substantial value you have acquired. Other owned assets of lesser value can be included in broad groups such as furniture, clothes, and so forth, without specifying individual items. To assist in identifying the assets you own, Figure 7 provides a selected list of the assets that are frequently owned by many individuals and families. You may find it useful to include other family members in helping to identify your assets and estimating their values.

FIGURE 7

Assets You May Own

Financial Assets	Tangible Assets
Cash	Home
Checking account	Other real estate
Savings account	Furniture
Certificates of deposit	Major appliances
Securities	Jewelry
Bonds	Silverware
Stocks	Collectibles (stamps, coins, art, etc.)
Mutual funds	Vehicles
Life insurance	Clothing
Retirement plans	Computers
Private pension plans	

You may need assistance in valuing some of your assets. When assets have modest values—say, $100 or less—approximations are not a great concern, and you can trust your own judgment of what the assets are worth. The following tips may help in valuing some of your major assets. Remember, you are trying to estimate the current amounts that your assets would bring if you were to sell them now, or if you decided to purchase similar items in comparable condition today.

Home

To obtain a ballpark valuation for your house or condo, see if you can come up with the price at which a similar home in your neighborhood was recently sold. If you don't mind being hassled a little, you can call a real estate brokerage firm and ask for a comparable valuation for your home. You might also consider calling the insurance agent who sold you a homeowner's policy for advice on your home's value. If you rent a home or an apartment, there will be no entry here.

Vehicles

Your cars, trucks, vans, or whatever else you drive are probably the next most valuable assets you own. If you don't own a home, a vehicle is likely to be your most valuable asset. It is often possible to obtain an approximate value for your car by scanning listings in the newspaper classifieds or advertisements placed by automobile dealers. If you locate an advertisement for a car similar to your own, you probably need to reduce the listed price by at least 10 percent to account for the likelihood that the quoted price is negotiable. If you are unable to locate an ad for a comparable car, call a credit union or bank and inquire about the wholesale and retail value of your car. Split the difference in determining the value of your vehicle. Be certain to take into account your vehicle's condition and mileage. You might also call the agent handling your automobile insurance, who should have a booklet that lists used car values.

> Subscribe to a local newspaper. Newspapers are the best source of information about products and prices. A careful reading of newspaper advertisements can produce substantial savings. Television and radio advertising provide little useful information for making intelligent shopping decisions.

Clip and save vendor coupons. Coupon in newspapers and magazines can easily save $300 to $500 per year in shopping costs. Sunday newspapers are especially valuable for coupon clippers.

Collectibles

If you are an avid collector of stamps, coins, baseball cards, or Elvis memorabilia, you probably have a good idea of the value of your collection. If you can't value what you own, then you almost surely have already been taken advantage of by other collectors to the point that you probably don't have much of value that remains. Other collectibles such as jewelry and silverware may require a professional appraisal. You are likely to need an appraisal of these items for insurance purposes, anyway.

Securities

Security values can frequently be determined by checking market prices in the financial pages of a major newspaper. The *Wall Street Journal* carries a more complete listing than do most daily newspapers. You may be unable to locate newspaper listings for some of your securities either because the securities did not trade on a particular day or because the securities trade only infrequently and are not regularly listed by the paper. If you own bonds or if you own stocks that are not actively traded, you will need to call a brokerage firm to determine the value of your securities. There should be no charge for this service. If your securities are kept in a brokerage account, the monthly statement you receive should list current market values for each security.

Mutual fund prices can be located in the financial section of many newspapers, or you can telephone the fund's sponsor.

Accounts at financial institutions

Certificates of deposit and savings accounts should be included at the values listed on the most recent monthly statements from the financial institutions that hold the funds. When listing your checking account balance, use the balance in your check register rather than the financial institution's monthly statement, because you are likely to have outstanding checks (checks you have written but that have not yet cleared your account) and, possibly, recent deposits that are not yet reflected in your statement. For example, you may have written several checks near the end of the month that either have not been presented to the bank for payment or were presented to the bank following the last day of the statement cycle.

Life insurance

Life insurance (if you have any) should be valued at the amount of money you would currently receive if you cashed in the policy. This means that only life insurance policies

Don't be in a hurry to buy something. The more you hurry a purchase, the more likely you are to buy something you don't need or pay too much for something you do need. Give yourself time to think about a purchase before you cough up the money. The more expensive the item being considered, the more time you should spend evaluating the purchase.

Eat at home. You can save substantial amounts of money by eating at home rather than dining out, even when you generally eat fast food. Restaurants typically pay about the same price as you for the food they purchase. They then mark prices up three or four times when they set menu prices. You are also likely to save some money on taxes, since most states tax restaurant meals but not groceries.

with a cash value should be included as assets. Do not make the mistake of valuing insurance policies at face value. The face value of a life insurance policy is applicable only when you die. Term insurance policies should not be included as assets because term insurance does not build cash values. If you have group life insurance with your employer or through some organization of which you are a member, the chances are that it is term insurance and should not be included as an asset. The longer life insurance policies with cash values have been in force, the greater the cash values will be. You can obtain the cash value of a life insurance policy by calling your insurance agent or by writing the company that issued the policy. Technically, other insurance policies—homeowner's insurance, auto insurance, and liability insurance—should be entered as assets to the extent that you have paid ahead. In practice you should not introduce this complication. Do not include these other insurance coverages as assets.

Employer retirement plan

If you have an employer-sponsored retirement plan, check with the personnel department or the plan's sponsor to determine the current value of your retirement benefits. You are attempting to determine the amount of money you would receive if you quit or retired as of the date of the balance sheet. The current value of your retirement plan will depend on several factors that vary among employers. For example, are you required to contribute to the plan, or does your employer fund the entire contribution? How many years of employment are required before you are "vested" in the retirement plan? That is, how many years are you required to work for your current employer before you can quit the job and still retain your retirement benefits? Determining the current value of your retirement plan may turn out to be one of the more difficult tasks of putting together your balance sheet.

Private pension plan

The current value of a private pension plan can be obtained from the plan's sponsor. You should receive periodic statements from the firm that administers an individual retirement account (IRA), a Keogh plan (if you have a similar one), or a similar retirement account. Other private retirement plans administered by an insurance company or some other financial institution should also send periodic reports. If you are unable to locate a recent report, write or call the plan's administrator.

Collecting Information About Your Debts

Unless your financial affairs are rather complicated, you should encounter less difficulty in identifying your debts and the outstanding balances you owe than you did in identifying and valuing your assets. First, you almost surely have fewer debts than assets. The smaller number of debts goes a long way in simplifying the process of identifying and valuing your liabilities. Second, there is generally no guessing required to determine the outstanding balance on a debt, so the dollar entries for debts should be more accurate than the dollar estimates for assets. Determining the outstanding balance on a loan normally requires a call or letter to the lender. The outstanding balance of the loan—the amount that you record as the current value of the debt—is the amount of money that is required to pay off the loan at the time you construct the balance sheet. Figure 8 is designed to help spur your memory with respect to the debts you might have.

Although it is generally not difficult to determine the outstanding balance on a loan, the tips below will provide some guidance if you run into a problem.

Home mortgage

The outstanding balance on your home mortgage (a *mortgage* is a real estate loan) can be obtained from the lender. Most home loans are structured with equal monthly payments for the life of the loan (this is termed an *amortized loan*), making it difficult to determine the extent to which the balance of the loan declines as you continue to make mortgage payments. For several years after you take out a home loan, a large proportion of each mortgage payment will be absorbed by interest being charged on the loan. The portion of each payment that goes to reduce the principal on the loan is quite small, so the outstanding balance of a long-term loan declines very slowly during the early years of the loan's life.

FIGURE 8

Debts You May Owe

Current bills
   Utility bills (electric, water, telephone, etc.)
   Debts to retailers
   Debts for services (TV repair, lawn care, etc.)
Charge cards (list each card separately)
Taxes
   Owed to the city and county
   Owed to the state
   Owed to the federal government
Personal loans
   Loans to individuals
   Unsecured loans to financial institutions
Auto loans
Other installment loans
Mortgage loans

Automobile loan

The outstanding balances of loans on your vehicles can be obtained by calling the lender. Like mortgage loans, most automobile loans are amortized and require equal monthly payments. When you call the lender, ask for the payoff on your loans. The payoff on the loan is *not* equal to the sum of all the remaining payments required on the loan. The payoff will depend on the length of time left on the loan.

FIGURE 9

1995 Balance Sheet for the Weaver Family

Assets		Liabilities and Net Worth	
Checking account	$ 1,375	Visa credit card	$ 470
Savings accounts	7,500	Department store #1 account	200
Stock	13,200	Department store #2 account	140
Furniture	3,000	First National loan	1,400
Clothing/personal	2,000	Auto loan	8,000
Automobile	10,000	Home mortgage	75,000
Retirement plan	8,000	**Total Liabilities**	**$ 85,210**
Home	95,000	Net Worth	$ 54,865
Total Assets	**$140,075**	**Total Liabilities and Net Worth**	**$140,075**

Credit cards

Credit card balances can be obtained from issuers of the cards. Do not use the balance on your last statement, because the information will be out of date. Recent charges on the card will not be included, and your last monthly payment may be omitted from the balance indicated on the statement. Be certain to account for recent changes that have not yet reached the card company. Most credit card issuers have toll-free telephone numbers for use by cardholders with questions. The number is likely to be imprinted on your card. If it is not, call the toll-free operator at 1–800–555–1212 and request the telephone number.

Personal loans

The outstanding balance on a personal loan can be obtained from the lender. The balances on some personal loans do not change because the loans require only periodic interest payments, so the loan's principal remains unchanged. For a personal loan on which you pay interest only, the outstanding balance is equal to the amount that was borrowed.

Your Net Worth

After you have totaled the current values of all your assets and calculated the amounts that are owed to each of your creditors, you can determine the dollar value of what you have been able to accumulate during your working life. Your net worth is the dollar value of your assets less the outstanding balances owed to your creditors. If you have no debts, then your net worth is equal to the current value of the assets you own. Wouldn't that be nice! Figure 9 provides an example of a balance sheet for the Weaver family, consisting of Steve, Sherry, and one child.

Your net worth should increase during most of your working years as increases in your assets exceed increases in your debts. Having a positive and increasing net worth is very important if you are to have any hope of attaining your established goals because these goals will require you to use your accumulated assets. When you begin to pay your son's college expenses, you will be consuming your acquired assets, thereby depleting your net worth. If your net worth is insufficient to support these expenditures, you will only be able to attain your goals by borrowing the difference.

Net worth will increase when there is an increase in the value of assets that you already own (for example, when your home appreciates in value or when there is an increase in the values of securities you own) and when you allocate a portion of your current income either to acquiring additional assets or to paying off a portion of your debts. Thus, you can increase your net worth by investing a portion of your current income rather than by spending all of your income on current needs.

CHAPTER 5

The Main Event: Putting Together Your Budget

A personal budget requires that you estimate your future income and future expenses. A comparison of these two estimates allows you to determine whether you can expect to experience financial shortages or surpluses in upcoming weeks and months. Practice is required to fine-tune your forecasts, but the estimates should become increasingly accurate as you gain experience. If the forecasts indicate that you will experience chronic deficits, it is time to review your planned expenditures and the goals you have established.

Establishing your budget—putting together estimated income, estimated expenses, and the periodic savings required to achieve the goals that you have identified—is the crux of this book. Many individuals encounter frustrations that cause them to throw in the towel in the early stages of developing a personal budget. Don't give up. Even though you may at times feel that your project has turned into a dismal failure, stick with it. You will find that the estimates gradually become more accurate at the same time that the budget consumes less of your time. The budgeting process will almost certainly require some fine-tuning of both expenses and goals, but the effort will produce worthwhile results.

Selecting a Budgeting Period

Before you begin the process of putting together a forecast, you must select a budgeting period. Do you want to budget every week, every other week, or once a month? People often choose a budgeting period that coincides with the frequency of their pay. For example, if you are paid every other week, you might find it most convenient to make forecasts and keep records for the same period. If you are paid monthly, you should probably choose a monthly budgeting period. The remainder of this chapter assumes a monthly budgeting period, but the same principles apply regardless of the budgeting period you choose.

Adjust your menus to grocery specials. It make financial sense to plan your menus around discounted grocery specials. Specials normally change weekly, so you can experience variety in your diet while you save on the grocery bills.

Forecasting Your Income

Most people find that estimating future income is the least complicated task in the preparation of a budget. Income estimation is especially easy when your only income is a wage or salary that varies little from one period to the next. If your employment produces a constant income, use the amount of your paycheck to project your wage income for each budgeting period. If you anticipate a salary increase in the near future, build the expected increase in income into your projections at the point that you expect the adjustment to take place.

If you earn an hourly wage from a job that involves wide swings in the amount of work you are able to get—say you work in construction or are employed part-time by several retail firms that offer varying hours of employment—you should combine a review of your past year's pay with your own forecast for the upcoming year. You may feel that the business environment will improve and that you will be offered additional hours of work during the coming year, for example. You are the person best able to judge your future employment and earnings. Remember, budget forecasts are not etched in stone, and you can revise any estimates after you begin the budget. Revisions are an important part of the budgeting process.

Estimates for either your gross pay (the amount you earn before deductions for such items as health insurance, social security, and federal and state income tax withholding) or your take-home pay (the net amount of your paycheck), whichever you prefer, can be used for the budget. Using gross pay requires you to provide estimates for each of the items that are deducted by your employer. Your employer's deductions are expenses that should be included in the expense section of the budget. Using gross pay and listing employer deductions will provide the greatest amount of detail in your budget, but it is probably easier, at least initially, to work with estimates for take-home pay rather than gross pay.

You may have sources of income in addition to a salary. In fact, you may have several sources of income but no salary. For example, you may earn interest from funds on deposit in a bank account, or you may receive dividends from stocks. Other possible sources of income include social security, rental income from property you own, and payments from a retirement plan. Figure 10 provides a list of potential income sources to assist in assembling a record of your own income.

Investment ownership will require that you estimate the income your investments will provide during each budgeting period. To refresh your memory concerning your investments and the income you can expect to earn in upcoming budgeting periods, examine your most recent federal tax return for the amounts of interest income and dividend income you reported. Next, determine the dates that investment income was earned by examining last year's bank deposits and brokerage account statements.

Ideally, next year's investment income will be somewhat greater than investment income earned during the past year.

Save lunch buckets of money by taking your lunch to work. It is much cheaper to eat a homemade lunch than to purchase a restaurant meal. You will also have an opportunity to accomplish some extra things (read the newspaper, for example) and eat healthier fare.

F I G U R E   1 0

Typical Income Sources

Net salary or wages (after deductions for income taxes withheld, social security, retirement plans, health insurance, and so forth)

Interest income from passbook savings accounts, checking accounts, market investment accounts, certificates of deposit, and so forth

Dividends

Social security

Retirement plan payments

Unemployment compensation

Rental income

Business income

Alimony or child support

Commissions, fees, bonuses, gifts, or tips

You may have accumulated a larger amount of savings in your bank account, or the companies whose stock you own may have increased their dividend payments. You may have made additional investments during the past year that should produce increased investment income in the coming year. Although some sources of income may be difficult to determine exactly, a little effort on your part should produce a relatively accurate estimate of future income in upcoming months.

Once you are satisfied with your estimates of future income and the dates the income will be received, it is time to enter the forecasts on your budgeting form. Figure 11 shows sample entries on a typical form for recording income forecasts. It is important to record each income source on a

FIGURE 11

Worksheet for Estimating Income

	January	February	March	April	May	June	July
Net Salaries							
Steve	$1,800	$1,800	$1,800	$1,800	$1,800	$1,800	$1,800
Sherry	500	400	550	500	700	800	800
Total	2,300	2,200	2,350	2,300	2,500	2,600	2,600
Interest							
First Federal	30	30	30	30	30	30	35
Credit Union			20			20	
Total	30	30	50	30	30	50	35
Dividends							
Exxon			128			128	
Gencorp		30			30		
Total	0	30	128	0	30	128	0
Total Income	$2,330	$2,260	$2,528	$2,330	$2,560	$2,778	$2,635

separate line to make it easier to identify and revise estimates as circumstances change. For example, the interest income may change when a certificate of deposit matures and the principal is reinvested in a new certificate that pays an interest rate different from the rate paid by the matured certificate. A different interest rate will change the amount of interest income you will earn and should cause you to revise your income estimates in upcoming budgeting periods.

When you are satisfied that you have identified all your income sources and you feel comfortable with the forecasts for each source, categorize each month's sources of income and total the amounts for each category. For example, total all salaries, all interest, all dividends, and so forth. You may end up with a forecast that comprises four or five income sources. If wages are your only income, there will be no other entries and no need to use categories in this section of the budget. The next step is to total all the income sources for each budgeting period. The totals for categories of income and the overall total income will be needed on a different form, which will be discussed later in this chapter.

Building a Record of Your Expenses

Expenses are often difficult to forecast, and the paperwork involved in this section of the budget can be a chore compared to keeping track of income. First, there are many more uses for your income than there are sources of income (as if you needed to be told). The large number of expenditures you make in any budgeting period—for gasoline, socks, lettuce, soap, a mortgage payment, video rentals, insurance, and so forth—makes it difficult to produce accurate estimates, at least initially. First, it is simply impossible to think of every product and service on which you will be spending money. Figure 12 provides a list of typical expenditures to help you construct your own list. Second, it may be difficult to determine the exact periods in which many of these expenditures will occur. How much will you be spending for the children's clothes in October as opposed to November? Third, you may be unsure exactly how much certain things will cost, especially for expenditures several months in the future. And then some costs are simply im-

FIGURE 12

Typical Expenditures

Fixed Expenditures	Flexible Expenditures
Rent/mortgage payment	Food
Auto loan payment	groceries
Personal loan payment	meals out
Insurance premiums	Clothing
automobile	Health expenses (unreimbursed)
disability income	dental
health	doctor
life	medicine
property	Transportation
Public transportation	repairs/maintenance
Education	gasoline
tuition	parking/miscellaneous
books/miscellaneous	Household expenses
Taxes	maintenance
property tax	furnishings
intangible tax	Utilities
estimated income tax	gas/oil
Goals	electricity
emergency fund	telephone
vacation	sewer and water
automobile	Personal care
college	Recreation
kitchen remodeling	Gifts
retirement	Charitable contributions

possible to predict. For example, will you be required to call a plumber during any of the budgeting periods?

With no information on which to base your forecasts, you are reduced to guessing at many of the budget's monthly expenditure forecasts. To keep the guesses from being too far off the mark, consider using the following two-step process.

1. *Review and categorize past expenditures.* Carefully review your check registers, receipts, and credit card statements to track at least a full year of past expenditures. The review should not be a quick once-over, but a detailed accounting of what happened to your income during each month of the past year. Every checkbook entry and credit card use is a piece of information that helps to reveal your spending pattern. Use this data to prepare a historical expense form similar to the one shown in Figure 13, in which columns are headed by sample spending categories. As you review spending records, transcribe each entry from your checkbook registers and credit card statements to the appropriate column. To simplify the record keeping, round all numbers to the nearest dollar.

Use a separate expenditure form for each month of the budget. Essentially, you are reconstructing each month's expenditures, by spending category, to produce a record on which to base your monthly spending forecasts. The spending record is useful for developing a forecast because spending in a given month is a good gauge of spending to be expected during that same month in the upcoming year. In other words, next January's spending is related to last January's spending, next February's spending is related to last February's spending, and so forth. Of course, if you recently

FIGURE 13

Expense Record for <u>October 1995</u>

Home Mort-gage	Utili-ties	Gro-ceries	Eating Out	Cloth-ing	Trans-porta-tion	Medi-cal	Insur-ance	Recre-ation	Per-sonal Care	Taxes	Educa-tion	Child Care	Miscel-laneous
$650	$96	$55	$17	$56	$27	$60	$200	$20	$15		$29	$115	$16
	38	14	6	29	19	35	115	6	12		121	12	6
	20	26	13	6	205	40		14	28			16	14
		15	24	17	19				17				17
		60	12	75	15								58
			16	35	116								12
			8	42									7
			27										16
			9										9
			12										22
			15										15
			6										6
			17										4
			14										
			24										
$650	$154	$170	$220	$260	$401	$135	$315	$40	$72	$0	$150	$143	$202

married or had another addition to your family, last year's spending record will be less helpful in producing forecasts.

All individuals who maintain personal budgets will not use the same spending categories. The categories you choose should depend on your own spending patterns. For example, if your employer pays every medical expense, there is no need for a medical expense category. Likewise, if you are single or married without children, there is no need for a child care spending category. You will have to review your own spending patterns to determine the things you purchase. The more money you spend in a particular category, the more likely it is that you should subdivide that category. For example, if you live in a large city, you may want to divide transportation expenses into "public transportation" and "auto expenses." Additional spending categories provide more information but will require more work on your part.

After you have completed the time-consuming but important review of your past expenditures, total each of the spending categories on each Monthly Expense Record and transfer these totals to a Historical Expense Record as shown in the June–October columns of Figure 14. The Historical Expense Record is similar to the final Budget Summary Sheet, which will be discussed later.

2. *Keep a record of current spending.* At the same time you are reviewing and categorizing past expenditures, begin

Make a list of the things you need to purchase before you go shopping. Retailers design their stores to sell you things you ordinarily wouldn't buy. Be prepared. Make a list of the things you intend to purchase and then stick with the list when you go shopping. Of course, if you find a *really* good deal . . .

FIGURE 14

Historical Expense Record

Expense Item	PAST					CURRENT	
	June	July	August	Sept.	Oct.	Nov.	Dec.
Home mortgage	$ 650	$ 650	$ 650	$ 650	$ 650	$ 650	$ 650
Utilities	160	175	190	160	154	162	171
Groceries	150	130	120	140	170	180	211
Eating out	120	130	140	170	220	120	165
Clothing	50	100	90	280	260	30	40
Transportation	330	290	280	320	401	273	317
Medical	20	90	—	60	135	70	45
Insurance	—	315	—	—	315	—	—
Recreation	50	65	170	50	40	50	90
Personal care	60	60	75	60	72	75	80
Taxes	—	—	—	—	—	—	550
Education	—	—	—	180	150	30	50
Child care	90	90	90	90	143	130	120
Household	40	49	20	70	50	47	60
Contributions to charity	300	—	—	300	—	—	600
Interest on credit cards	—	—	—	—	—	10	15
Emergency fund	120	90	80	100	100	100	75
Miscellaneous	150	120	221	180	202	174	517
Total	$2,290	$2,354	$2,126	$2,810	$3,062	$2,101	$3,756

keeping a detailed record of your current spending. A record of the amounts you are currently spending for groceries, clothing, gasoline, and so forth is a second source on which to forecast the size and timing of future expenditures. The review of your checkbook and credit card statements should provide an accurate record of most expenditures, but there are certain to be some gaps in this information. For example, you may have written many checks for cash, in which case it will be difficult to determine how a substantial amount of your income was spent. Monitoring several months of current spending should help fill these gaps and provide improved data on which to base your spending forecasts.

FIGURE 15

Expenditure Notebook

	Groceries	Oct.
10/5	Food Lion	$55
10/12	Winn-Dixie	14
10/15	Winn-Dixie	26
10/20	Kroger	15
10/26	Winn-Dixie	60

To maintain a record of current spending, carry a small notebook and record the date, item purchased, and amount spent each time you pull out your billfold, checkbook, or credit card. The information will be easier to analyze if you allocate separate pages in the notebook for each spending category. In other words, set aside a page for groceries, a page for clothing, a page for auto expenses, and so forth. A page in your notebook might look like Figure 15. Initially, it is preferable to include too many rather than too few categories. Little-used categories can eventually be combined or consolidated with other major categories. Be sure that each entry includes enough information so that you can later refer to the notations and understand what they represent.

When you have gained a feel for your current spending habits (say, after several budgeting periods), total the amounts in each spending category and transfer the totals to the Historical Expense Record you are using to record past spending (as shown in the months of November and December in Figure 14). Now compare your current spending record for November and December with the historical spending pattern for June through October that emerged from the review of past spending. This comparison will help identify omissions from your historical spending review.

The record keeping required to produce an accurate esti-

Buy nongrocery items at a discount store, rather than a grocery store. Grocery stores offer low prices on groceries but generally charge relatively high prices for nongrocery items such as beauty aids. Buy soap, detergent, toothpaste, and brooms at a discount store such as Kmart or Wal-Mart, not at the local supermarket or convenience store.

mate of your current spending is probably the biggest chore of the budgeting process. Still, you need to determine the amounts of money you are spending and how the money is being spent. Tracking expenditures during this information-gathering period is good practice for the actual budgeting process, when you must record current expenditures to compare with your forecasts.

Estimating Your Expenses

With a record of past expenditures, you are ready to forecast future expenditures. Some financial planners suggest that you divide expenditures into two broad categories: expenditures that are fixed and expenditures that are flexible. Fixed expenditures remain relatively constant from one budgeting period to the next. Examples of fixed expenditures include mortgage or rent payments, installment loan payments, life insurance premiums, automobile insurance premiums, and required savings to meet your established goals. A fixed expense can occur each period (such as mortgage or auto loan payments) or only occasionally (life insurance premiums that are paid annually and automobile insurance premiums that are paid quarterly or semiannually).

Flexible expenses vary in amount from one budgeting period to the next and, as a result, are difficult to forecast. On the positive side, you are able to influence the amounts that are spent in flexible expense categories, so this section of the budget presents an opportunity for some useful planning. For example, a spending category for "eating out" should be included in the flexible expense section because the amounts spent for eating out are influenced by many different fac-

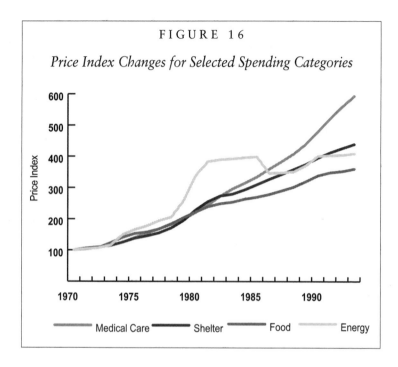

FIGURE 16

Price Index Changes for Selected Spending Categories

Medical Care   Shelter   Food   Energy

tors, causing these expenditures to vary widely from period to period. At the same time, you should be able to maintain a large degree of control over the amount of money that is spent in a given budgeting period for restaurant meals.

The expenditure forecast should consider inflation, especially if your estimates are being made during a period of rapidly rising prices. In projecting health insurance premiums for more than a single year, for example, you can probably count on your premiums being higher next year than this year. During periods of relatively stable prices, incorporating a factor for inflation is less important, especially if your forecasts are for a year or less. Although rate of inflation can be used to project expenditures, the various categories of spending seldom change to the same degree. Figure 16 illustrates the differences in price shifts since 1970 in four categories of expenditures.

Fixed expenses

Begin your expenditure forecast with estimates for fixed expenses that are relatively easy to determine. The amounts and timing of most of your upcoming insurance premiums should be apparent. Likewise, last year's property tax bill can be used to determine the approximate amount of the tax in the upcoming year. If there is reason to expect an increase in the property tax, call your local taxing authority and request an estimate of the next assessment. Required monthly payments on outstanding loans and periodic amounts that must be set aside to meet your identified goals should be included as fixed expenses. All these expenditures should be relatively easy to forecast for each budgeting period in the year ahead.

Fixed expenses that are less certain can be estimated by using the spending data collected during the past year. If you believe that some of these expenditures will remain at approximately the same level in the upcoming year, use last year's totals, adjusted for expected inflation, for your entries

---

Periodically check the tire pressure of your vehicles. Underinflated tires wear poorly and result in poor gas mileage for your vehicle. Maintaining correct tire pressure is a painless way to save money. A good tire-pressure gauge is an investment that will earn high returns.

on the Budget Summary Sheet. Inflation adjustments are calculated by multiplying last year's spending by one plus the expected inflation rate. For example, if you spent $120 in a particular spending category last March and expect an annual inflation rate of 5 percent, the forecast for next March in this spending category is $120 times 1.05, or $126.

Flexible expenses

Flexible expenditures are more difficult to forecast than are fixed expenditures. Flexible expenditures tend to vary, sometimes substantially, from one budgeting period to the next, making it difficult to estimate the amount of each month's spending. The best method for forecasting flexible expenditures is to review last year's spending record and to use similar amounts for your forecasts in respective budgeting periods in the year ahead. For example, if you spent $140 for groceries last March, you should forecast grocery spending of a little more than $140 (to account for inflation) for March of the coming year.

As you forecast expenditures, keep in mind that some spending categories exhibit seasonal variations. For example, you may incur large clothing expenditures each fall and each spring. It is also likely that you experience higher utility bills during certain months or seasons of the year. Spending trends should become evident as you review the

Maintaining a good attitude is an important part of the budgeting process. A halfhearted attempt at a budget is almost surely doomed to failure. Budgeting isn't exciting or particularly fun, but it can help you improve your financial condition.

record of your past expenditures. Seasonal variations in spending mean that you cannot simply average an entire year's expenditures for a particular spending category and come up with an accurate weekly or monthly forecast.

How to Incorporate
Debt Payments into the Budget

Required payments on outstanding loans should be built into the expenditure forecast. For example, if you are making monthly car or installment-loan payments, you should include each of these required payments on a separate line in the expenditure section. If several loans are outstanding, you may want to incorporate a section for loan payments. Ideally, a substantial reduction or even an elimination of the entries in this category will occur several years into the budget process.

To handle outstanding loans that don't have a large required payment (for example, a credit card balance that requires only a nominal minimum payment), work out a payment plan that will allow you to pay off the loan balance on a specific date. For example, establish a series of fixed payments for each of your credit card balances so that the loans will be paid off at a certain point in the future. If the budget is effective, your future borrowing will be curtailed, and you will eventually be able to delete this category of spending.

Do not double-count expenditures by including spending for items that are purchased on credit as well as the payments that will be required to pay off the debt. You should only include one or the other. The problem with using loan payments—especially payments on credit card balances—is that you lose track of which categories of spending are consuming your income. The best advice is to incorporate loan payments on borrowing you have already incurred but use only the regular categories for purchases that are forecast for future months. Take control of your financial affairs and stop buying on credit!

The Need for Revisions

Changes in your life are likely to necessitate adjustments to your forecasts. Modifications in the composition of your budgeting unit (marriage, a child leaving for college, divorce, and so forth) will have a major impact on your spending pattern and will necessitate substantial revisions to your forecasts. Major changes in your life may also necessitate modifications to your income forecasts.

Revisions to your expenditure forecasts will also be necessary to adjust for more usual changes, such as an altered inflation outlook and small adjustments in your spending patterns. For example, a sudden change in inflationary expectations may be occasioned by a disruption in energy supplies. This change may affect your budget forecast for utilities and transportation. You should remain sufficiently flexible to be able to adjust your estimates.

Revisions to your forecasts are most likely to be needed during the early stages of your budget, when you are still feeling your way. As you gain experience, the forecasts will become more accurate and fewer revisions will be needed.

Combining Forecasts of Income and Expenditure

When you are satisfied with your forecasts of periodic income and spending, transfer the forecast amounts to a budget summary form similar to the one shown in Figure 17. The information on this form will serve as the summary statement for your budget. The summary statement contains all your forecasts and all the actual income and spending data for each period. This data will indicate how closely your actual income and spending track the forecasts you have made.

The summary form that you use does not have to be identical to Figure 17. If you have decided to use a large number of spending or income categories, you are likely to need separate forms for expenditures and income. The desire to list certain categories of income will depend in large part on the sources of your income. If you earn substantial amounts of income from dividend payments and from a retirement plan, you will need a separate line for each of these items. On the other hand, if you have only small amounts of income other than your salary, you may decide that a single "other income" entry on the summary budget form is satisfactory.

Accept the fact that you can't afford everything you want. You must be willing to give up some things in order to get other things. A budget will identify what you can and can't afford. Being forced to choose in advance is likely to result in an improved standard of living.

FIGURE 17

Budget Summary Sheet

	JANUARY			FEBRUARY		
	Actual	Forecast	Difference	Actual	Forecast	Difference
Income						
Salary—Steve	$1,800	$1,800	$ 0	$1,800	$1,800	$ 0
Salary—Sherry	1,000	500	500	800	400	400
Interest	30	30	0	30	30	0
Dividends	0	0	0	30	30	0
Total Income	$2,830	$2,330	$500	$2,660	$2,260	$400
Fixed Expenses						
W/D fund	$ 100	$ 100	$ 0	$ 100	$ 100	$ 0
Auto fund	200	250	(50)	250	250	0
Vacation fund	22	50	(28)	50	50	0
Gen. savings	0	50	(50)	131	50	81
Emergency fund	100	100	0	100	100	0
Home mortgage	650	650	0	650	650	0
Utilities	170	150	20	162	175	(13)
Insurance	296	280	16	0	0	0
Taxes	0	0	0	90	95	(5)
Education	25	20	5	30	25	5
Child care	90	85	5	90	85	5
Flexible Expenses						
Groceries	$ 170	$ 150	$ 20	$ 160	$ 150	$ 10
Eating out	150	125	25	140	125	15
Clothing	0	50	(50)	40	50	(10)
Transportation	376	300	76	303	300	3
Medical	187	60	127	45	60	(15)
Recreation	40	30	10	50	30	20
Personal care	75	60	15	67	60	7
Household	40	30	10	51	30	21
Contributions to charity	0	0	0	0	0	0
Interest on credit cards	18	15	3	14	10	4
Miscellaneous	121	100	21	137	100	37
Total Expenses	$2,830	$2,655	$175	$2,660	$2,495	$165

After entering income and spending forecasts, calculate the total of your expected income sources and the total of your planned spending categories for each budgeting period. If the totals indicate that expenditures will exceed income in most of the upcoming periods, you obviously have a problem. For example, the January forecast in Figure 17 shows that spending is expected to exceed income by $2,655 minus $2,330, or $325. The February forecast projects a somewhat lower deficit. Possible solutions include a review of spending plans with the goal of reducing planned expenditures, a review of income forecasts with a goal of increasing your sources of income, or an acceptance that you will be borrowing increasing amounts of money to support spending that is in excess of income. You may decide to use a combination of two or all three of these.

Comparing forecasts of future income and spending is likely to force you to face some hard choices about your future finances. Until this point you have been formulating spending plans without concern for the amount of income that will be available. Now you must view spending in light of the limited amounts of money that will be available to support the planned expenditures. Welcome to the real world.

The first step following a forecast that indicates chronic deficits is to review your goals and decide which ones are really important and which ones are merely desirable. Given the expectations relative to your financial resources, you may want to prune some of the goals that now appear impossible to attain. Another possible solution is to delay the implementation of some goals in order to reduce the amount of saving that is required each period. For example, you might push back by a year the purchase of a new car in order to reduce the amount that must be put aside each period to pay for it. Smaller periodic savings would then be required because you now have an additional year to meet the goal. Yet another possible solution is to downsize several of your goals. You may decide to buy a less expensive car or to take a shorter vacation. Don't fret about having to alter your goals. It is better to make these changes early than to wait until later and be surprised by your inability to attain the goals.

A forecast of deficit spending may necessitate a review of both past and planned spending in order to identify individual expenditures and categories of expenditures that can be trimmed. The spending review may indicate that you can achieve substantial savings both by eating out less often and by cutting back on amounts you tend to spend for clothing. Chats with neighbors may reveal that your electric bills are substantially higher than the bills of families who reside in similar homes. These new insights will allow you to revise downward the amounts forecast for each of these spending categories. Of course, you must follow up by also reducing your spending in categories you have revised downward. Only you, along with other members of your family, will know which categories of spending can be reduced with the least amount of pain.

Evaluating Your Forecasts

The Budget Summary Sheet in Figure 17 contains a column for recording each period's actual spending and actual income. Placing the forecast amounts and actual amounts side by side allows for a convenient check of the accuracy of your forecasts. You have already determined the amounts that you expect to earn and how much you plan to spend each period in each category. You have struggled to bring your forecast spending into balance with your expected income. The next step is to compare these forecasts with the amounts you actually earn and spend. When you worked with forecast amounts, your intentions and forecasting skills mattered. When you use actual amounts, it is your actions that matter.

You must continue to maintain a written record of your expenditures as long as a personal budget is maintained, so don't throw away your notebook! At the end of each budgeting period, total all the expenditures in your notebook for each spending category and record each category's total on the budget summary form. For example, total all your expenditures during the period for groceries and copy this total under the appropriate column and on the appropriate line of the summary budget form. Now you can compare the amount you planned to spend on groceries with the amount that you actually spent on groceries. Continue to transfer information from your notebook until you have completed the column for actual expenditures in the appropriate budgeting period.

The third and last column in each budgeting period is for recording the difference between the actual amount and the forecast amount for each spending and income category. For

Continuously evaluate your insurance needs. Many individuals waste money by purchasing insurance that is inappropriate with respect to both type and amount. Don't waste money paying for insurance you no longer need.

example, suppose you forecast $140 for restaurant meals in February. If you actually spend $165 for meals during the month, $25 would be recorded in the difference column to indicate the amount by which you *overspent* in this category. On the other hand, if you only spend $85 eating out during the month, you would enter $55 in parentheses to indicate that you *underspent* your forecast by $55. The difference column calls attention to categories in which you are spending substantially more or less than you anticipated. Overspending or underspending in a category on a regular basis indicates that you have faulty forecasts that need to be revised. In Figure 17, the "Difference" column for income sources is interpreted in a similar manner. A positive number represents greater income than forecast, and a number in parentheses represents less income than forecast.

Steve and Sherry's budget summary in Figure 17 forecasts deficits (expenditures that exceed income) for both January and February. The couple forecasts January expenditures of $2,655, $325 more than anticipated income for the month. A somewhat smaller deficit of $235 is forecast in February. Steve and Sherry have carefully reviewed their spending plans and the forecasts in Figure 17 reflect reductions they have made in several spending categories. Despite these reductions, the budget forecasts deficits for each of the two months.

Think about canceling collision and comprehensive insurance on an older vehicle. The amount of money you would collect from a settlement for a loss may not be worth the premiums you would be required to pay.

Notice that Steve and Sherry decided to included five categories of saving in the expense section of their budget. They feel that they are more likely to achieve the goals they have established (see the goals in Figure 6 of Chapter 3) if the monthly saving required to attain the goals is entered in this section of the budget. Incorporating saving as an expense places saving on an equal footing with entertainment, food, utilities, and every other expense category. You may find in preparing your own budget that it is more convenient and understandable to include saving in a separate section from expenses. That's fine. Keep in mind that most financial experts suggest that you specifically budget for saving rather than allow saving to sop up whatever funds happen to remain after all other spending needs are met. Treating saving as a residual tends to lead to no saving.

Steve and Sherry can handle the planned deficit in one or a combination of several ways. They can follow the path of least resistance and settle for a reduced amount of saving in each month. For example, they can attempt to balance January's budget by saving $325 less than planned. Choosing this alternative makes it less likely that all of the goals they have established will be achieved. Another possibility is to borrow the difference so that monthly saving goals can be met. Choosing to borrow postpones the day of reckoning, unless the deficit is expected to be temporary.

A third choice is to further reduce planned expenditures. For example, the couple could plan to quit eating out for the next several months. This would increase their outlays for groceries somewhat, but should result in increased monthly saving of $100 or so. Likewise, they could postpone clothing expenditures until later in the year. A fourth choice—the option selected by Steve and Sherry—is to balance the budget by earning additional income. The couple decided that Sherry would attempt to find additional work so that extra income would be available to meet the spending forecasts. The availability of more work was uncertain and the added income is not included in the January and February income forecasts of Figure 17.

The actual income entries in Figure 17 indicate that Sherry was able to earn additional after-tax income of $500 in January and $400 in February. Thus, actual income substantially exceeded forecast income in both months. If the increase in income was the only change that occurred, the couple would have a balanced budget. In fact, they would have realized a surplus. Unfortunately, actual expenditures exceeded anticipated expenses for both months. Entries in the January "Difference" column indicate that actual expenditures were higher than anticipated in more than half of the spending categories. The forecasts seriously underestimated spending for transportation and medical care. Because of the higher spending in January, Steve and Sherry were able to make the full allocation only to the savings fund for a new washer and dryer and to the emergency fund. They were unable to meet target savings for the auto fund, the vacation fund, and the general savings fund. The February forecasts were more accurate. Although actual spending exceeded forecasts in several categories, Sherry's $400 of extra income (together with overestimated expenses in four categories) allowed the couple to meet each of February's monthly saving goals. The surplus was allocated to the general savings fund, although it could just as well been used to make up the previous month's shortfall in two other savings funds.

It appears that Steve and Sherry are likely to encounter a similar financial squeeze in subsequent months. If spending continues at current levels, additional income will be required on a monthly basis. Thus, since they expect no increase in unearned income, either Steve or Sherry or both will need to find higher-paying employment or face the fact that they will have to work additional hours. Alternatively, they could reexamine the goals they have established, which appear to be unrealistic and hence need to be redefined. They may decide to drop the general savings fund and the vacation fund. Or they could scale back the proposed outlay for an auto by accepting a used vehicle in place of a new one.

The bottom line is that although the numbers in the budget summary don't present a particularly pretty picture, they force Steve and Sherry to face an expected financial squeeze before they sink in a sea of debt. Being able to pinpoint the areas where they are facing financial difficulties will allow them to take corrective action before things get out of hand.

The early stages of a budget are almost certain to produce large discrepancies between your forecast expenditures and the amounts you actually spend. The discrepancies will probably be less pronounced in the income section, where forecasts tend to be more accurate. Don't become discouraged by inaccurate forecasts; they are a common problem for anyone who initiates a budget. View the differences as valuable information that will help you make a more accu-

---

Beware of investments that offer unusually high returns. High returns generally indicate high risk. Be wary of anyone who tries to sell you on an investment that is "guaranteed" to provide a higher return than you could reasonably expect to earn anywhere else.

FIGURE 18

*Average Monthly Cost of Food at Home
for Food Plans at Four Cost Levels, 1994*

Family Size	Thrifty	Low-cost	Moderate	Liberal
Individuals				
Male (age 20–50)	$107.80	$137.70	$173.00	$209.60
Male (51 and over)	97.50	131.50	162.40	194.60
Female (age 20–50)	97.00	121.50	147.70	188.90
Female (51 and over)	95.80	117.70	145.80	174.40
Families				
Family of 2 (ages 20–50)	225.30	285.10	352.80	438.40
Family of 2 (51 and over)	212.60	274.10	339.00	405.90
Family of 4				
Children ages 1–5	328.40	410.70	502.70	617.80
Children ages 6–11	376.30	482.70	604.10	727.00

Source: Agricultural Research Service, U.S. Department of Agriculture, *USDA Family Food Plans (Oct. 1994)*

rate budget. The inaccurate forecasts indicate particular areas in which you don't realize how much you are spending. Spotlighting this discrepancy allows you to readjust your life-style in an attempt to reign in spending. Figure 18 and Figure 19 may help you to forecast your spending.

Figure 18 shows estimated average food costs in September 1994 for providing nutritious meals for family units of different sizes. The four food plans listed represent spending by individuals and by family units at different income levels. The information in Figure 18 is useful for determining the initial amount of your budget for food expenses. You can

FIGURE 19

*Typical Expenditure Patterns
by Income Classification, 1992*

Item	Annual Income Before Taxes		
	$5,000 to $9,999	$20,000 to $29,999	$50,000 to $69,999
Food at home	$ 1,666	$ 2,558	$ 3,562
Food away from home	509	1,406	2,712
Tobacco and alcohol	319	621	815
Shelter	2,661	4,576	7,941
Household operations and supplies	413	715	1,411
Utilities, fuels, and pub. services	1,349	1,859	2,559
Household furnishings	357	1,020	1,856
Apparel	636	1,564	2,780
Private transportation	1,555	4,672	7,675
Public transportation	97	233	439
Health care	1,046	1,648	2,087
Personal care products	181	377	604
Entertainment	436	1,159	2,679
Education/reading	277	325	878
Miscellaneous	283	637	1,224
Cash contributions	191	688	1,421
Personal insurance/pensions	284	2,013	6,152
Total annual expenditures	$12,260	$26,071	$46,795

Source: Bureau of Labor Statistics, U.S. Department of Labor, *Consumer Expenditures in 1992*

also compare these estimated expenditures for food with the amounts you actually spend in order to determine if your spending is in line with the cost of providing a nutritious diet.

Figure 19 contains data showing how typical families in different income classes allocate their income to various spending categories. When viewing the expenditures for each income class, be aware that your own spending patterns will vary from those shown, perhaps substantially, simply because of where you live and how your family is structured. In other words, don't feel guilty if you spend more or less in a particular spending category than the amount indicated in Figure 19.

The Budget as an Ongoing Project

Most people who initiate a personal budget will find a need to indefinitely continue the process. A personal budget is much like a diet; if you don't continue the effort, your financial condition (as opposed to your physical condition) will almost surely revert to the same state that preceded the implementation. In the case of discontinuing a diet, you may revert to uncontrolled eating and an expanding posterior. If you discontinue a budget, you will regress to your previous life-style of undisciplined spending.

Many people have honorable intentions when they undertake a personal budget, but they are either too lazy to continue, or they don't like the discipline that a budget imposes. The truth is that a budget "tells it like it is," and many individuals don't like to be faced with the realization that they can't have everything they want.

If you start to think about discontinuing the budget, remind yourself that maintaining a budget will allow you to obtain the greatest enjoyment that your income can support on a continuing basis. A budget keeps you from frittering away money on things that don't matter so that more money will be available for things and activities that do matter. The budget introduces reasoning to your spending, and this helps you spend your money more intelligently.

As you gain experience in maintaining a budget, you will almost surely develop methods to economize on your effort. For example, you are likely to find it convenient to bunch several kinds of spending into a miscellaneous category. Your expenditures on odds and ends such as snacks and small personal items will probably consume a similar amount of income each budgeting period. Rather than continue to estimate and record all these small expenses each budgeting period, simply assume that your forecast is accurate and record actual spending equal to forecast spending in the miscellaneous category. The reduction in effort is worth the small discrepancy in the spending record that will result. Don't implement this technique, however, until you have accumulated enough data to make a reasonably accurate forecast for miscellaneous spending.

CHAPTER 6

Using a Computer for Personal Budgeting

Using spreadsheet software on a computer can help remove some of the drudgery of constructing the various documents associated with the budgeting process. In addition to saving time, a computer can help ensure that the information is more accurate, more comprehensive, and easier to read, store, retrieve, and display. Computerizing your budget also facilitates revisions of income and expenses. Using Lotus 1-2-3, this chapter explains how a spreadsheet program can be used to prepare personal financial statements on a computer. Commercial software for better money management is available at low cost.

NOTE: This chapter was written by Dr. Kent Moore, Professor of Management and Information Systems at Valdosta State University (and a devoted Elvis fan).

Admittedly, preparing balance sheets, income and expense records, and budgets can become somewhat time-consuming and tedious. A computer can help by making it easier to organize and store information. Also, the computer can do many of the required calculations, and the results can be printed in a more attractive format.

A *spreadsheet*, also sometimes referred to as a *worksheet*, is a two-dimensional table with rows and columns. Spreadsheet software programs are easy to learn and to use. Some of the most widely used spreadsheet programs are Lotus 1-2-3, Quattro Pro, and Excel. In this chapter Version 2.01 of Lotus 1-2-3 is used, but other versions of 1-2-3 or other spreadsheet programs can be used with only minor modifications. ("Lotus 1-2-3" is a registered trademark of the Lotus Development Corporation.)

Constructing a Balance Sheet Using a Spreadsheet

First, review Figure 9 (page 58) and suppose that the balance sheet was computed for December 31, 1995. Columns of a spreadsheet are denoted by letters, and rows are denoted by numbers. The titles of the asset accounts, the numerical values of the asset accounts, the titles of the liability and net worth accounts, and the numerical values of the liability and net worth accounts will be placed in columns A, B, D, E, respectively, of the spreadsheet shown in Figure 20. The default (standard) column width for Lotus 1-2-3 is nine characters, but column widths can be increased to accommodate longer account titles. The procedure for increasing the width of Column A to twenty characters is to place the cursor anywhere in Column A and press /, Work-sheet, Column, Set-Width, 20. Column D should be widened in the same manner. The sums for total assets, total liabilities, and total liabilities and net worth can be calculated automatically by noting which rows are to be totaled and using the @SUM function. For example, the formula for 1995 total assets in cell B17 would be @SUM(B8..B15), and the formula for 1995 total liabilities in cell E15 would be @SUM(E8..E13). The formula for 1995 total liabilities and net worth in cell E19 could be written as +E15+E17. The plus sign preceding the formula is necessary to signal Lotus 1-2-3 that the item in the cell is a numerical value rather than an alphabetic label. It is a good idea to state the amount in cell E19 in terms of previous cell addresses, instead of using specific numerical expressions like 85,210 + 54,865. This allows for automatic recalculation if numbers later need to be changed. Also, it is important to remember that 1-2-3 formulas must not contain spaces between characters.

You will want to construct a new balance sheet periodically (at least once a year) to determine how your financial standing has changed. Suppose that you now want to construct a balance sheet for December 31, 1996, using data that you have just collected. These 1996 figures will be entered alongside the 1995 figures in columns C and F. This enables you to compare the two years and see clearly the change that has occurred in each item. Checking and sav-

> Don't commit your savings to an investment you don't understand. An investment that is beyond your understanding is likely to entail risks you don't want to face.

FIGURE 20

1995 and 1996 Balance Sheets

Row	Column A	Column B	Column C	Column D	Column E	Column F
		1995	1996	Liabilities and Net Worth	1995	1996
6	Assets					
8	Checking account	$ 1,375	$ 1,700	Visa credit card	$ 470	$ 650
9	Savings accounts	7,500	8,000	Dept. store #1	200	250
10	Stock	13,200	13,400	Dept. store #2	140	160
11	Furniture	3,000	2,800	First National loan	1,400	900
12	Clothing/personal	2,000	2,100	Auto loan	8,000	6,000
13	Automobile	10,000	7,500	Home mortgage	75,000	73,500
14	Retirement plan	8,000	9,000			
15	Home	95,000	97,000	Total liabilities	$85,210	$81,460
17	Total assets	$140,075	$141,500	Net worth	54,865	60,040
19				Total Liabilities and Net Worth	$140,075	$141,500

ings accounts have increased, automobile value has decreased, auto loan and home mortgage have decreased, and so forth. Most important, the net worth of the Weaver family has increased from $54,865 to $60,040, which is encouraging.

To print a spreadsheet such as the balance sheet in Figure 20, use the following steps. First, place the cursor in the upper-left corner of the area you wish to print, for example, cell A1. Then press /, Print, Printer, and Range. Next, to anchor the beginning of the area to be shaded, type a period after the words "Enter Print Range: A1," which are displayed on the screen. Now use the right arrow to move to Column F and the down arrow to move to Row 19. This designates the range to be printed, namely cells A1 through F19. Last, press Go to accomplish the printing.

There are three options for constructing a balance sheet for 1997. You could enter the new 1997 amounts in columns B and E by typing over the 1995 amounts. A second way is to insert a blank column after Column C (which moves the information in columns D–F to columns E–G) and use a new column (H) at the far right. The 1997 figures could then be entered in columns D and H alongside the 1995 and 1996 figures. The procedure for inserting a new column between columns C and D is to place the cursor anywhere in Column D and then press /, Worksheet, Insert, Column, and the return key. This approach, of course, would enable you to compare changes in each item for three years.

A third variation may be the best of all. As years are added, the balance sheet becomes too wide for a standard sheet of paper. The entire Liabilities and Net Worth section could be moved below the Assets section by marking a block and using the Lotus 1-2-3 Move command. The resulting vertical arrangement would provide room for several years of balance sheet data. To accomplish this move, first place the cursor in cell D6. Then type /, select Move, and in response to "Enter Range to Move From," type a period to anchor the upper-left corner of the range. Next move the cursor across to cell F6 and down to cell F19 and press the return key to mark the entire range. In response to "Enter Range to Move To," move the cursor to cell A22 and press the return key. The entire Liabilities and Net Worth section of the balance sheet will then be moved from the area D6–F19 to A22–C35.

Income Worksheets

A spreadsheet program is even handier for constructing income and expense records. First, we will look at a Worksheet for Estimating Income, similar to the one in Figure 11 (see page 66). An extension of Figure 11 that goes through December is shown in Figure 21. When several cells have the same numerical value, the Lotus 1-2-3 Copy command is a real convenience. For example, since Steve's salary is a constant $1,800 from January through July, $1,800 can be entered once in cell B10 and then copied into cells C10–H10. To accomplish this, first place the cursor in cell

Wash your clothes in cold water. Clothes will last longer when washed in cold water (hot water weakens fabrics) and your energy bill will be lower. The hot water heater is one of your home's biggest energy users.

B10. Then type /, select Copy, and hit the return key to enter the range From: B10..B10. Then move the cursor to cell C10, and the range specification "To: C10" will appear automatically. Type a period to anchor the left end of the shaded area and move the cursor to cell H10, which results in "To: C10..H10" showing on the screen. Pressing the return key will then complete the copying. The interest income from First Federal, which is a constant $30 from January through June and then $35 monthly for the rest of the year, can be handled in a similar way. Now suppose Steve knows that he will get a 6 percent raise beginning in August. In cell I10 enter 1.06*B10, and the new salary of $1,908 will automatically be calculated. This salary can then be copied into the columns for September through December. As usual, totals for all columns can be automatically calculated by indicating which specific cells should be summed. For example, the formula for March total income in cell D29 would be +D13+D20+D27.

Annual Totals and Monthly Averages

Two new columns, Total and Average, have been added to Figure 21 in columns N and O. Because the spreadsheet is now so wide, it is inconvenient to scroll back and forth from the titles and early months to the later months and summary figures. More important, when you are looking at the later months, it is difficult to keep in mind which rows correspond to which categories because the titles are no longer visible on the screen. You can improve this situation with the following steps. Move the cursor to anywhere in the January column and use these strokes: /, Worksheet, Ti-

FIGURE 21

Worksheet for Estimating Income

Row	Column A	B	C	D	E	F	G
6	Source	Jan.	Feb.	Mar.	Apr.	May	June
8	*Net Salaries*						
10	Steve	1,800	1,800	1,800	1,800	1,800	1,800
11	Sherry	500	400	550	500	700	800
13	Total Salaries	2,300	2,200	2,350	2,300	2,500	2,600
15	*Interest*						
17	First Federal	30	30	30	30	30	30
18	Credit Union			20			20
20	Total Interest	30	30	50	30	30	50
22	*Dividends*						
24	Exxon			128			128
25	Gencorp		30			30	
27	Total Dividends	0	30	128	0	30	128
29	**Total Income**	2,330	2,260	2,528	2,330	2,560	2,778

FIGURE 21 *(continued)*

Worksheet for Estimating Income

H	I	J	K	L	M	N	O
July	Aug.	Sept.	Oct.	Nov.	Dec.	Total	Ave.
1,800	1,908	1,908	1,908	1,908	1,908	22,140	1,845
800	750	750	850	850	900	8,350	696
2,600	2,658	2,658	2,758	2,758	2,808	30,490	2,541
35	35	35	35	35	35	390	32
		20			20	80	7
35	35	55	35	35	55	470	39
		142			142	540	45
	25			25		110	9
0	25	142	0	25	142	650	54
2,635	2,718	2,855	2,793	2,818	3,005	31,610	2,634

tles, and Vertical. This fixes Column A so that it does not scroll. Now move the cursor to the Total column and you will notice that you can see both the latter columns and the category titles.

To total the annual income in each category, first go to cell N10 and enter @SUM(B10..M10), which will automatically calculate Steve's annual net salary. Sherry's annual net salary in cell N11 would be calculated using @SUM (B11..M11) and, similarly, totals could be computed for the other rows. Alternatively, the formula in cell N10 could be copied into cell N11 by using /, Copy, From: N10..N10, To: N11..N11. Note that the formula is automatically changed from @SUM(B10..M10) to @SUM(B11..N11) when it is copied. This "relative copying" feature will be explained in more detail later. Notice also that the total in cell N29 could be done by summing Column N or by summing Row 29. This is a helpful check on the accuracy of your work.

Next, in the Average column, you will use the Lotus 1-2-3 @AVG function. First, however, you will reformat so that the averages will be rounded and displayed as whole numbers rather than as decimals. Column O alone could be reformatted, but since you want to use only whole numbers throughout, you will reformat the entire spreadsheet with this sequence of commands: /, Worksheet, Global, Format, Fixed, 0 decimal places. To calculate the monthly averages

---

View the time you spend on maintaining a personal budget as an investment. The savings you are able to produce per hour spent on this task is likely to exceed the hourly income you earn from employment.

in each income category, enter @AVG(B10..M10) in cell O10, @AVG(B11..M11) in cell O11, and so on. Alternatively, cell O10 could be calculated using +N10/12, and so forth. cell O29 can be calculated using +O13+O20+O27 or by using +N29/12, which again provides a check. (A minor difference could occur due to rounding.)

Expense Records

The amounts in a monthly expense record (see Figure 13, page 70) come from entries in an expenditure notebook like the example shown in Figure 15, page 73, from check stubs, receipts, and so forth. Entries in a monthly expense record could be entered each day as they occur. It would probably be easier, however, to put entries in an expenditure notebook or to collect and store receipts for a while and then periodically enter the information. At those times the information could be transcribed to a monthly expense record on paper or put in a monthly expense record spreadsheet. An advantage of a computer spreadsheet like the one in Figure 22 is that the @SUM function can be used to maintain current totals for all expense categories.

Particularly early in the budgeting process, you may have expenses in new categories that you had not thought about. New columns can be inserted as needed to handle these new categories. For example, suppose you have just purchased a nice $58 birthday gift for your wife in October and you are aware that Christmas gifts will be purchased in the near future. Rather than put this expenditure in the Miscellaneous category, you decide to add a new category, Gifts, and you would like to place it between Transportation and Medical.

FIGURE 22

A Portion of the Monthly Expense Record
for October 1995

Row	Column A Mort.	B Util.	C Groc.	D Eating Out	E Clothing	F Transp.	G Gifts	H Med.	I Insur.
8	650	96	55	17	56	27	58	60	200
9		38	14	6	29	19		35	115
10		20	26	13	6	205		40	
11			15	24	17	19			
12			60	12	75	15			
13				16	35	116			
14				8	42				
15				27					
16				9					
17				12					
18				15					
19				6					
20				17					
21				14					
22				24					
27	650	154	170	220	260	401	58	135	315

A new column can be placed there by placing the cursor in Column G (Medical) and using the commands /, Worksheet, Insert, and Column, as explained earlier. Now Gifts becomes Column G, Medical becomes Column H (instead of G), Insurance becomes Column I (instead of H), and so forth, as shown in Figure 22. If a new column is inserted after @SUM commands for previous columns have been entered, those commands are automatically changed to reflect the new columns. For example, the total for Medical is changed from an expression of the form @SUM (G8..G26) to @SUM(H8..H26). Notice that the @SUM command was placed in Row 27 to allow room for additional entries. The row in which the totals appear could be moved up or down, by deleting or inserting blank rows, as necessary.

In the Historical Expense Record (Figure 14, page 72), the amounts for each item are, of course, taken from the column totals in the Monthly Expense Record (Figure 13). For example, note that the $154 expenditure for utilities in October is shown as the total of the second column in the Monthly Expense Record for October and also is the October entry in the second row of the Historical Expense Record. The @SUM function can be used to calculate the total expenses for each month (column totals) and also the annual expenses for each budget category (row totals). Both these sets of totals provide important information. You need to know your total expenditures for each month, and you also need to know how much you are spending in each budget category for the year.

The expenses for June–December that were shown in Figure 14 are shown again in Figure 23. In addition Figure 23 includes expenses for the rest of the year, and two new columns, Total and Average, have been added as columns N

FIGURE 23

Historical Expense Record

Row	Column A	B	C	D	E	F	G
6	Expense Item	Jan.	Feb.	Mar.	Apr.	May	June
8	Home Mortgage	650	650	650	650	650	650
9	Utilities	150	182	151	142	134	160
10	Groceries	190	140	160	155	155	150
11	Eating Out	150	140	140	130	130	120
12	Clothing		40		75		50
13	Transportation	356	323	320	345	340	330
14	Gifts						
15	Medical	187	45	110	50	35	20
16	Insurance	296			296		
17	Recreation	40	50	30	25	40	50
18	Personal Care	95	47	50	65	55	60
19	Taxes		90		412		
20	Education	30	25	20	15	60	
21	Child Care	90	90	90	90	98	90
22	Household	35	56	30	40	50	40
23	Contributions to Charity			300			300
24	Interest on Credit Cards	18	14	11	8	5	
25	Emergency Fund	50	70	100	100	100	120
26	Miscellaneous	121	137	145	157	161	150
29	**Total Expenses**	2,458	2,099	2,307	2,755	2,013	2,290

FIGURE 23 *(continued)*

Historical Expense Record

H	I	J	K	L	M	N	O
July	Aug.	Sept.	Oct.	Nov.	Dec.	Total	Ave.
650	650	650	650	650	650	7,800	650
175	190	160	154	162	171	1,931	161
130	120	140	170	180	211	1,901	158
130	140	170	220	120	165	1,755	146
100	90	280	260	30	40	965	80
290	280	320	401	273	317	3,895	325
			58		314	372	31
90		60	135	70	45	847	71
315			315			1,222	102
65	170	50	40	50	90	700	58
60	75	60	72	75	80	794	66
					550	1,052	88
		180	150	30	50	560	47
90	90	90	143	130	120	1,211	101
49	20	70	50	47	60	547	46
		300			600	1,500	125
				10	15	81	7
90	80	100	100	100	75	1,085	90
120	221	180	202	174	517	2,285	190
2,354	2,126	2,810	3,120	2,101	4,070	30,503	2,542

and O. To calculate the annual totals for each expense category, first go to cell N8 and enter @SUM(B8..M8) to get the annual home mortgage amount. Then copy the formula @SUM(B8..M8) to cells N9 through N26 by using / Copy, From: N8..N8, and To: N9..N26. The rest of the row totals will then be calculated immediately. This is indeed a powerful feature of Lotus 1-2-3 and other spreadsheet programs. With just a few keystrokes, the annual totals are calculated for all nineteen expense categories. This is made possible by "relative copying"; that is, Lotus 1-2-3 copies formulas but alters the formulas relative to their new locations (states them in terms of their new rows or columns). So the formula @SUM(B8..M8) in cell N8 automatically becomes @SUM(B9..M9)in cell N9, @SUM(B10..M10) in cell N10, and so forth. The monthly (column) totals and the calculations in the Average column are done in a similar manner. For the monthly totals enter @SUM(B8..B26) in cell B29 and then copy the formula to cells C29 through N29. For the averages, in cell O8, enter @AVG(B8..M8) and then copy this formula to cells O9 through O26. Cell N29 should have the same answer whether you sum Column N or you sum Row 29, and cell O29 should have the same answer whether you sum Column O or divide cell N29 by 12. It is good policy to do cells N29 and O29 both ways to check that the figures are correct.

The annual totals and monthly averages provide valuable information. Averages are useful, for example, in determining the amounts you need to set aside monthly for expenses that occur only periodically, such as taxes and insurance. Infrequent expenses have a tendency to sneak up on you when you think that your finances are in good shape. Because insurance costs an average of $102 per month, that amount should be set aside each month in order to be able to cover the bills of $296 and $315 when they come due.

Either the averages or the totals are instructive in another way. Both are measures of the amounts you have been spending, but perhaps the monthly averages are easier to relate to. At the end of the year, you should compare your monthly net income with your average monthly expenses. The Weaver family did rather well, as you can see by comparing the results in the lower right of Figure 21 and Figure 23. The Weaver's average monthly income was $2,634, and their average monthly expenses were $2,511. If you are like many American families, however, your expenses exceeded your income. If so, you are living beyond your means, and you need to either increase your income or decrease your expenses. Increasing your income may be difficult or impossible; thus, it is likely that a reduction in expenses should be implemented. Don't subscribe to the "I'd rather not know this" idea, or the "ignorance is bliss" theory. Also, don't view the budgeting process and the resulting knowledge of expenses as punishment, but rather as information that can be used as a basis for sound actions.

Budget Summary Sheets

Before deciding which expenses to reduce, let's look at one more thing. In Figure 17 (page 82), a Budget Summary Sheet indicates the differences for two months between budgeted and actual income and expenditures. This information is converted to a spreadsheet in Figure 24. The Copy command can be used to calculate the differences quickly. First, enter all the actual and forecast amounts for January and

FIGURE 24

Budget Summary Sheet

	Column A	B	C	D	E	F	G
Row 6			January			February	
8		Actual	Forecast	Diff.	Actual	Forecast	Diff.
10	*Fixed Expenses*						
12	Emergency Fund	100	100	0	100	100	0
13	Home Mortgage	650	650	0	650	650	0
14	Utilities	170	150	20	162	175	−13
15	Insurance	296	280	16	0	0	0
16	Taxes	0	0	0	90	95	−5
17	Education	25	20	5	30	25	5
18	Child Care	90	85	5	90	85	5
19	Saving	322	450	−128	531	450	81
20	*Flexible Expenses*						
22	Groceries	170	150	20	160	150	10
23	Eating Out	150	125	25	140	125	15
24	Clothing	0	50	−50	40	50	−10
25	Transportation	376	300	76	303	300	3
26	Medical	187	60	127	45	60	−15
27	Recreation	40	30	10	50	30	20
28	Personal Care	75	60	15	67	60	7
29	Household	40	30	10	51	30	21
30	Contributions to Charity	0	0	0	0	0	0
31	Interest on Credit Cards	18	15	3	14	10	4
32	Miscellaneous	121	100	21	137	100	37
34	**Total Expenses**	2,830	2,655	175	2,660	2,495	165

FIGURE 24 *(continued)*

Budget Summary Sheet

Column A	B	C	D	E	F	G
Row						
6		January			February	
8	Actual	Forecast	Diff.	Actual	Forecast	Diff.
37 *Income Sources*						
39 *Net Salaries*						
41 Steve	1,800	1,800	0	1,800	1,800	0
42 Sherry	1,000	500	500	800	400	400
43 Total Salaries	2,800	2,300	5000	2,600	2,200	400
45 *Interest*						
47 First Federal	30	30	0	30	30	0
48 Credit Union	0	0	0	0	0	0
49 Total Interest	30	30	0	30	30	0
51 *Dividends*						
53 Exxon	0	0	0	0	0	0
54 Gencorp	0	0	0	30	30	0
55 Total Dividends	0	0	0	30	30	0
56 Total Income	2,830	2,330	500	2,660	2,260	400

February in columns B, C, E, and F. Then in cell D12 enter the formula +B12–C12. Next, copy the formula from D12 to cells D13 through D19 and copy it again from D12 to D22 through D32. Your spreadsheet now will automatically calculate all differences between actual and forecast expenses for January. Similarly, enter the formula +E12–F12 in cell G12 and then cony it from G12 to G13 through G19 and G22 through G32 to obtain the differences for all expense items in February. As a check, cell D34 should equal the difference between cells B34 and C34, and cell G34 should equal the difference between cells E34 and F34. Positive differences represent items for which you spent more than you forecast, and negative differences represent items for which you spent less than you forecast. The data entries for the income sources in rows 41 through 54 are handled in a similar manner. On this portion of the Budget Summary Sheet, positive differences represent income sources from which you earned more than the amount forecast, and negative differences represent sources that produced less income than the amount forecast (no such negative differences are shown in Figure 24).

Spend some time looking at the items that were underbudgeted or overbudgeted. The budget for future periods should be brought more in line with actual expenses. It may simply be that the budget was incorrect and that the forecast amounts need to be changed to the actual expenditures for past periods, with some adjustments for inflation or anticipated future changes in spending patterns. On the other hand, it may be that too much was spent in those categories that were underbudgeted. If so, rather than change the budget, these categories are good candidates for places to cut expenditures.

Graphs of Expenditures

In accordance with the saying "A picture is worth a thousand words," you may wish to construct some graphical representations of your expenditures for the past budgeting period. Lotus 1-2-3 has graphics as well as spreadsheet capabilities. First, it would be desirable to arrange the expense categories in order of magnitude from largest to smallest, except for Miscellaneous, which could be left as the last category, as shown in Figure 25. This rearrangement is a good suggestion for next year's budget process, whether or not you intend to draw graphs, because it helps you see more clearly where your money goes. Another change has occurred in Figure 25. In order to make the graphs less cluttered, the number of expense categories has been reduced by consolidating some categories, as shown in Column C. Home Mortgage, Utilities, and Household have been combined into Housing; Groceries and Eating Out are combined into Food; Taxes and Insurance are consolidated; Child Care and Education are put together; Gifts, Interest on Credit Cards, and Miscellaneous are grouped under Other. Abbreviations and amounts for the new categories are shown in columns D and E. To highlight the manner in which the Weavers are spending money, all saving other than for the emergency fund has been omitted from Figure 25 and from Figure 26. Saving can easily be included if desired.

Now let's draw a bar graph to display the amounts for each of the various expense categories. Using the data in the spreadsheet shown in Figure 25, the commands for constructing the bar graph in Figure 26 are as follows. First, be sure that the spreadsheet itself is saved by using /, File, and Save, and entering a file name, for example, EXH66. Now

FIGURE 25

Average Monthly Expenses

	Column A	B	C	D	E
Row					
6	Expense Category	Amount	Revised Category	Abbrev	Amount
8	Home Mortgage	650	Housing	Hous	857
9	Transportation	325	Transportation	Trans	325
10	Utilities	161	Food	Food	304
11	Groceries	158	Taxes & Insurance	Tx & In	190
12	Eating Out	146	Child Care & Education	Ch & Ed	148
13	Contributions to Charity	125	Contribution to Charity	Contr	125
14	Insurance	102	Emergency Fund	Emerg	90
15	Child Care	101	Clothing	Cloth	80
16	Emergency Fund	90	Medical	Med	71
17	Taxes	88	Personal Care	Pers	66
18	Clothing	80	Recreation	Recr	58
19	Medical	71	Other	Other	197
20	Personal Care	66			
21	Recreation	58			
22	Education	47			
23	Household	46			
24	Gifts	31			
25	Interest on Credit Cards	7			
26	Miscellaneous	159			
29	**Total Expenses**	**2,511**			

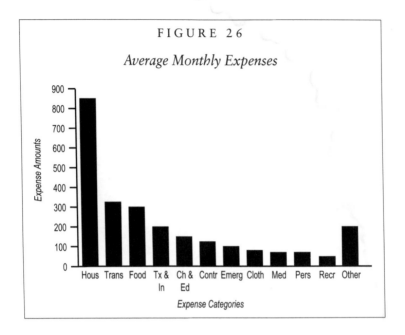

FIGURE 26

Average Monthly Expenses

press /, Graph, and Type, and select Bar. Then select X and set the X-axis Range as D8..D19 by putting the cursor at cell D8, typing a period, and moving down to cell D19. If necessary, use the ESC key to allow you to move to D8. Also, use the ESC key any time you need to back up to the previous menu. Select A and set the First Data Range as E8..E19. Next, press Options and Titles. For the First Title (overall graph title), enter Average Monthly Expenses. For the X-axis and Y-axis Titles, respectively, enter Expense Categories and Expense Amounts. Press View if you want to see the graph on the screen. Then type Save and store it under a file name, say EXH67BAR. To print the graph, exit the main 1-2-3 program, return to the opening menu, and

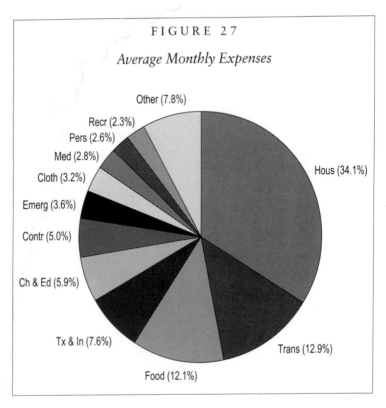

FIGURE 27

Average Monthly Expenses

select PrintGraph. For Image-Select choose EXH67BAR and press Go, which initiates the printing process.

Pie charts are helpful for visualizing the relative amounts spent for each of the categories. The pie chart in Figure 27 is based on the data in Figure 25, and it shows each expense category as a percentage of total expenditures. The commands for constructing the pie chart are identical to the ones above except under Type, select Pie instead of Bar. Name it EXH68PIE and again print it from the PrintGraph program.

Now, back to the matter of reducing expenditures, if necessary. Look at the amounts shown in Figure 23 (Historical Expense Record). If your average monthly expense is greater than your average monthly income, then you probably need to cut expenses for the following year. There are two exceptions: (1) You expect a substantive increase in income next year; or (2) you have extraordinary expenses in one or more categories (for example, hospitalization costs) that are not expected to occur again next year. Be aware, however, that some new expenses (home or auto repairs, for instance) may come along next year. Which expense categories appear too large? Which expense reductions would cause the least pain or hardship? Would you rather eat out less frequently or have a shorter vacation? Would you rather drive an older car or buy fewer new clothes? As indicated earlier, the budgeting process helps give you the information necessary for making these sometimes difficult choices and for avoiding more serious financial problems in the future.

Few people consider the budgeting process to be fun. A computerized spreadsheet such as Lotus 1-2-3, however, makes the process quicker, more accurate, and less of a hassle. Hang in there; the rewards can be great.

Commercial Computer Software

Many commercial software programs have been developed for individuals who do not have the knowledge, interest, or time to develop their own computer spreadsheet program. Most of these programs are modestly priced, especially compared to high-powered spreadsheet, data base, and word-processing programs. The cheapest prices are generally those offered by mail-order firms that advertise heavily in computer magazines. The best-known money management program, Quicken, by Intuit, is regularly sold by mail-order firms from under $50. Perfectly adequate money management computer shareware programs are available for no cost from computer bulletin boards. These same programs can be purchased for only a few dollars from commercial firms.

Commercial software and shareware programs offer the advantage of immediate use—after you have learned to use the program, of course. In other words, a spreadsheet similar to the one discussed in this chapter has already been constructed. You merely plug in the numbers. Commercial software contains bells and whistles such as colorful graphics, attractive screen layouts, and added functions (for instance, check writing and organization of tax information) that would be difficult to develop yourself.

The downside to many commercial programs is the amount of time and effort it takes to become proficient. Some complicated programs take weeks or months to learn. The developers have improved in this area, however, especially in the case of software such as money management programs that are aimed at the masses. All in all, computers help rather than hurt when putting together your budget.

> If you nearly always pay your monthly credit card bill in full, use a credit card that doesn't have an annual fee. You needn't care about the rate of interest that is charged on unpaid balances if you pay the full amount of your bill each month.

CHAPTER 7

What to Do with Your Savings

An understanding of how to invest your savings is an important part of personal budgeting. A budget requires that you set aside funds in order to attain goals that you or your family have established. You must know what kinds of investments are available and understand which of these investments are most suitable for meeting a particular goal. Before putting money into an investment, you should have an understanding of the risks that are inherent in owning the investment. This chapter discusses the various investments that are available along with the suitability of these investments for meeting certain types of goals.

You do not need the financial knowledge of a professional investment adviser in order to make intelligent investment decisions, although there is a certain amount of understanding you should acquire before investing your money. It is important to be able to assess the risks that are applicable in owning a particular investment, for example. Likewise, you should have some understanding of the returns an investment can provide and the regularity with which the returns can be expected to occur. Some investments have the potential to produce very high rates of return, but the returns might exhibit substantial variations from one year to the next. A high variability of returns makes the investment unsuitable for meeting certain goals.

Make an effort to learn the basic characteristics of a variety of investment vehicles. At the very least, you should have some knowledge of stocks, bonds, mutual funds, and products offered by commercial banks and savings and loan associations. The more you can learn about various investment vehicles, the greater the number of options you have for investing your funds. If you know only about certificates of deposit, you are likely to stick with this investment and forgo the advantages of owning other types of investments.

The Risks of Investing

The risk of owning an investment asset stems from an uncertainty of the return you will earn. The less certain the return you will earn from a particular investment, the more risk there is to owning that investment. Owning an insured certificate of deposit with a three-month maturity entails little risk because you know exactly how much interest income you will earn and the date the principal will be returned. On the other hand, having part ownership in a small business causes you to face substantial uncertainty relative to the returns you may earn, even though the returns could turn out to be quite high.

Investments may produce uncertain returns for several reasons. One possibility is that an organization in which you have invested will be financially unable to make the payments you expect. For example, a company may become short of cash and decide to eliminate dividend payments to its owners. Another possibility is that unexpectedly high inflation will eat away the purchasing power of the payments you do receive. If you invest in a long-term certificate of deposit just before a prolonged and unexpected burst of inflation, you will receive the expected payments of interest and principal, but they will be worth substantially less than you had anticipated.

Some investments are risky to own because the investments can be difficult to convert into cash. You may suddenly need funds and discover that you must pay a penalty or accept a reduced price to redeem or sell the investment. Other investments produce uncertain cash payments. For example, you may find yourself reinvesting funds from a matured certificate of deposit at a reduced return because of a decline in interest rates. There are many risks that investors

Establish an emergency fund that you can dip into in the event you become ill, unemployed, or have some large, unexpected expense. High liquidity and safety of principal are important requirements for any investment that is to serve as an emergency fund.

face, and unless you understand what these risks are, your investment program may produce some major surprises.

Why Different Goals Dictate Different Investments

Goals differ in importance and in the length of time before they are to be acheived. A short-term goal is best attained by using short-term investments. It is very risky to invest in common stocks or long-term bonds when you will need the funds in a year or two. Likewise, investing only in six-month certificates of deposit in order to accumulate funds for retirement is unduly conservative and likely to result in lower returns than could have been earned by holding a variety of other investments.

Conservative investments (investments with fairly predictable returns) should be used to attain your most important goals. This is true whether the goals are long-term or short-term. For example, high-quality investments are appropriate to hold for the short-term goal of an adequate emergency fund. Likewise, a family should avoid high-risk investments for accumulating a retirement fund, especially if retirement is anticipated within a decade. On the other hand, an expensive vacation is likely to be judged as something that would be enjoyable but not necessary; as

Ask your credit card company to waive the annual fee or to reduce the interest rate on your account. Credit card companies are hungry for business and will often agree to one of the two requests, but only if you ask. Why should they lower the price of their product if you continue to use the card without inquiring?

a result, you might feel more comfortable using high-risk investments to fund the trip.

Investments Appropriate to Short-term Goals

Short-run goals are best served by investments with substantial price stability and a high degree of liquidity. That is, investments used to attain short-term goals should have a predictable value and be easy to convert into cash without loss of value. Anything can be sold if the price is right. For short-term goals you should choose investments that retain their value when they are converted into cash.

Assets with a high degree of liquidity usually earn relatively low rates of return. Thus, the cost of choosing a liquid asset is a rate of return that probably isn't much higher than the rate of inflation. Investments with great liquidity tend to be very safe, but you can't get rich owning them. (Although, if you are already rich and have enough money invested in these assets, you can stay rich.)

Checking and savings accounts

Checking and savings accounts at insured financial institutions offer the ultimate in safety and liquidity. The principal of your investment is insured by an agency of the federal government, and you can obtain your money without penalty whenever it is needed. These accounts differ somewhat from one institution to the next. Savings and loan associations often offer slightly higher returns than commercial banks do. Credit unions frequently offer interest rates that are even higher than the rates paid by savings and loans. Financial institutions have widely varying policies for checking accounts. It pays to shop among several institutions before opening either a checking account or a savings account.

Several methods can be used to calculate the interest that is paid to account holders, so two institutions quoting the same rate of interest may end up paying a different dollar amount of interest for identical deposits. Some institutions pay interest on the low balance of the month, whereas other institutions pay interest from day of deposit to day of withdrawal; and some institutions pay interest on less than the entire balance in an account.

Financial institutions frequently levy charges on an account if you fail to maintain a specified minimum balance. Again, it is worthwhile to shop around for the institution that offers the most favorable terms, including the lowest required minimum balance. If the institution where you have an account changes its rules, don't allow inertia to keep you from checking out competing institutions to determine if you can get a better deal elsewhere.

Balances in checking and savings accounts should be kept at a low level. Maintain the minimum amount that allows you to pay your bills promptly. You should also maintain a balance that is slightly higher than the required amount to avoid a monthly service charge. The bottom line is that checking and savings accounts are generally not good investment vehicles for meeting even short-term goals.

Money market deposit accounts

Money market accounts offered by deposit-type financial institutions (banks, savings and loans, credit unions) can be good investment vehicles for meeting short-term goals. Insured money market accounts are very safe with respect to your knowing that principal and interest will be there when you need it. Also, there is no concern about a variation in the market value of your principal or about having to liquidate the investment at a discount. You always know the exact value of the account, and you can access funds in the account either by cash withdrawals or by writing checks.

An important risk for someone with funds invested in a money market deposit account is the possibility of reduced income caused by falling interest rates. This risk is particularly important for individuals who invest in a money market account to meet long-term goals or who depend on the investment to provide a stable current income. Money market accounts are satisfactory investments when a potential reduction in interest income is not such an important risk. For example, if you are saving for next summer's vacation, a reduction in the interest paid on the funds you have set aside will not turn into a disaster.

The return on a money market account is established by the individual financial institution holding the account; thus, one institution may pay a return that is higher than the return paid by another institution located nearby. Because of differences in interest rates paid on money market deposit

---

Don't buy shares of a mutual funds until you check on the fees. Many mutual funds charge a sales fee or a redemption fee, two charges you can easily avoid by choosing the appropriate fund. Also, check on annual management fees, which vary from .3 percent to 1.5 percent of assets. Fees can take a big bite out of your investment in a mutual fund.

accounts, it is a good idea to shop among institutions. The funds are easy to transfer or withdraw, so you don't have to worry much about not getting the best deal when you choose your initial account. There is nothing wrong with opening a money market account by mail with an out-of-town institution when you are unable to locate a local institution that pays a competitive return.

Money market funds

A money market fund is a special type of mutual fund (mutual funds will be explored later in this chapter) that limits its investments to high-quality, short-term financial instruments such as U.S. Treasury bills and large certificates of deposit. A money market fund pays for its management expenses with a portion of the income that is earned from the fund's investments. The fund then passes on the remainder of the income to investors. Hundreds of money market funds are in operation, each paying somewhat different returns because each fund invests in different securities and charges different management fees. It pays an investor who is interested in putting funds into a money market fund to investigate fees and historical returns.

Ownership of a money market fund is different from ownership of a money market deposit account. First, money invested in money market funds is not insured in the same manner as money deposited in money market accounts. On the positive side, money market funds invest primarily in high-quality securities, and certain money market funds restrict their investments to instruments of the U.S. Treasury. Money market funds also offer a greater variety of investment opportunities than money market accounts do. For example, some money market funds invest only in short-term tax-exempt securities in order to provide their shareholders with tax-exempt income.

Returns paid by money market funds are more responsive to changes in market interest rates than are interest rates paid on money market deposit accounts. For example, when short-term interest rates are rising, money market funds will tend to pay higher returns than money market deposit accounts. The difference in returns makes it advantageous to move your funds from one type of account to another, depending on the relative returns that can be earned. Both investments allow withdrawals by check, so transfers are easily arranged.

U.S. Treasury bills

U.S. Treasury bills are a popular investment among institutions and wealthy individuals. The problem facing individual investors is that Treasury bills are purchased and traded in a minimum denomination of $10,000 and multiples of $5,000 above that. Thus, you must be able to invest a substantial amount of money to consider owning Treasury bills.

Think twice about purchasing an extended warranty. An extended warranty is likely to be a good deal if you are a heavy user of a product, but a bad deal if you are a light user of the product. For example, if you generally put few miles on a vehicle, you may want to skip buying the extended warranty. Likewise, if you live alone or if you and your spouse have no children, you may want to skip the extended warranty on a new washer and dryer.

Treasury bills can be purchased directly from the Federal Reserve (instructions for direct purchases are available by mail from the Federal Reserve) or, for a nominal fee, through a commercial bank or brokerage firm. New bills with maturities of thirteen and twenty-six weeks are auctioned each Monday, and bills with a one-year maturity are auctioned monthly. Bills are sold at a discount from face value, and interest is earned on the difference between the discounted price that an investor pays and the face value that is returned at maturity.

Treasury bills provide returns that are approximately the same as the returns that can be earned from investing in a money market account or a money market fund. Interest income from Treasury bills is not subject to state taxes but is subject to federal taxes.

An active secondary market exists for Treasury bills, so the securities are easy to resell prior to maturity. There is no guarantee of the price you will obtain when a bill is sold, but short-term Treasuries vary little in price because principal is returned so soon (that is, the maturity is so short).

Investments Appropriate to Long-term Goals

Investors are faced with a great variety of investment opportunities to meet long-term goals. Common stocks, preferred stocks, corporate bonds, U.S. government bonds, mutual funds, a private business, and rental property are some of the investments that can be used to attain long-term goals.

When funds will not be needed for many years, there is less reason to be concerned about variations in the market value of an investment. For example, bonds with long maturities vary substantially more in price than bonds with short maturities do. These price variations should be of great concern if you may need to draw on the funds within a couple of years. Variations in the value of an investment are far less worrisome when you are putting funds aside to attain a long-term goal. If you are saving to achieve a long-term goal, you can accept short- and intermediate-term price variations in return for a boost in the expected rate of return.

Common stocks

Common stock represents ownership in a business. The more successful the business, the greater the firm's value, and the greater the value of the stock. On the other hand, the stock of an unsuccessful company is likely to decline in price and, if a company actually fails, the stock may end up having no value at all.

Common stock can be a very risky investment, and individuals sometimes lose substantial sums of money investing in shares of common stock. Common stocks are not homogeneous investments, and risk can vary significantly from one common stock to the next. For example, investing in the stock of an established firm that has a long record of consistent earnings and dividends involves much less risk

Realize that you are giving up the purchase of something when you buy something. A vacation may mean you wait an extra year before trading cars, and eating out a lot may mean a week less vacation time. You only have so much money available and spending some of it on one thing means that the same money won't be available to spend on something else.

than investing in a firm that is just being formed or a firm that operates in an emerging industry.

Common stocks produce two kinds of income for investors—increased stock value and dividends—both of which depend on profits. A firm's profits can be reinvested in additional assets that will produce even more profits in subsequent years. Thus, a firm's reinvested earnings normally result in an increased value for its common stock. Stock that you purchase for $25 per share in 1996 may increase in value to $47 per share five or six years later. Of course if a firm's managers make faulty decisions and invest in assets that fail to produce additional income, the common stock of the firm may actually decline.

Companies often pay a portion of earnings to stockholders in dividends, a second source of income for an investor in common stocks. Companies that pay a high portion of their earnings in dividends have less money available to invest in new assets. The stocks of these companies are generally purchased for current dividend income rather than for the appreciation in their expected price. Conversely, the stocks of companies that pay little or no dividends are generally purchased for an anticipated appreciation in value rather than for current income.

It is difficult even for investment professionals to consistently and accurately judge the future performance of a business. As a result, individuals who purchase common stocks should spread their investments among a number of different companies. Unless a person has a considerable amount of money available to invest, this diversification is difficult to accomplish when individual issues of stock are purchased. The solution may be to invest in mutual funds, an investment that will be addressed shortly.

Bonds

Bonds are long-term debt securities that are issued by corporations, cities, countries, states, U.S. government agencies, the U.S. Treasury, and foreign governments. A bond's interest payments and redemption date are established at the date of issue. Suppose a bond issued by Cincinnati Bell specifies an interest rate of 8 percent and a maturity date of December 15, 2005. Interest payments on the bond are calculated as 8 percent of the bond's $1,000 face amount (corporate bonds are denominated in $1,000 amounts), or $80 per year. Actually, interest is paid semiannually, so a bondholder would receive payments of $40 per bond each six months. The payments will remain the same regardless of whether market rates of interest increase or decrease following the date the Cincinnati Bell bonds are issued.

Bonds are appropriate investments primarily for individuals who seek a steady source of income. If you purchase $5,000 worth of high-quality bonds with a 9 percent interest rate and a ten-year maturity, you are virtually assured of receiving $450 annually for ten years, at which time the $5,000 principal amount will be paid. You should never purchase a bond without first checking the bond's credit quality.

Although bonds are a good source of current income, these securities have a limited potential to increase in value. The fixed interest payments cause a bond to change in market value when there are changes in market rates of interest. For example, a bond that pays $80 in annual interest is no longer worth $1,000 when new bonds of equal maturity and quality are paying annual interest of $95. In other words, when market rates of interest rise, there is a decline in the market values of bonds that are already outstanding.

Conversely, when market rates of interest decline, there will be an increase in the prices of outstanding bonds. More than anything else, market rates of interest drive the market values of outstanding bonds. The longer the time until a bond matures, the more the market value of the bond is affected by changes in market rates of interest.

Municipal bonds—debt securities issued by cities, counties, and states—are of particular interest to individuals with income subject to high tax rates because most of these securities pay interest that is free of federal and, often, state and local income taxes. Municipal bonds pay interest rates that are lower than the rates available on either corporate or U.S. government bonds, but because municipal bond interest payments are exempt from taxation, the after-tax returns from owning them may be higher than the returns from owning taxable bonds. You should avoid purchasing municipal bonds unless you pay income taxes at a relatively high rate.

U.S. Savings Bonds

There are two kinds of U.S. Savings Bonds available to individual investors. Series EE Savings Bonds are issued at prices equal to half their face value with an original maturity of twelve years. Denominations of $50, $75, $100, $200, $500, $1,000, $5,000, and $10,000 are available. An indi-

---

Don't buy trendy clothes. The more trendy the threads you buy, the sooner you are likely to discontinue wearing them. Conservative clothes tend to have a long life because they remain in fashion for a longer period.

vidual can purchase a $500 Savings Bond for $250, a $1,000 Savings Bond for $500, and so forth.

Series HH Savings Bonds are issued only in exchange for Series E/EE Bonds with redemption values that total $500 or more. Series HH Bonds are issued and redeemed at face value and pay current semiannual interest (that is, interest is paid each six months by electronic funds transfer).

Series EE Bonds held at least five years earn interest that, subject to a minimum level, is equal to 85 percent of the average yield on five-year Treasury securities during the time the bond is held. Thus, the interest rate earned on Series EE Savings Bonds changes with variations in market rates of interest. The interest rate on Series HH Savings Bonds is fixed at the time of purchase. For current rate information on U.S. Savings Bonds, call 1–800–US–BONDS.

Savings Bonds offer several investment advantages. First, interest earned on both Series EE and Series HH Bonds is exempt from state and local (but not federal) taxation. Second, reporting interest income from Series EE Bonds can be deferred until the bonds are cashed. Third, interest income from U.S. Savings Bonds purchased after December 31, 1989, may be exempt from federal income tax if the proceeds are used to pay tuition and fees at institutions of higher education. There are certain restrictions on this exemption, including a phaseout of the benefit for taxpayers with incomes above stipulated levels.

Mutual funds

Mutual funds are companies that invest your money in securities. Rather than invest in factories and equipment to manufacture some product, a mutual fund purchases stocks and bonds in an attempt to earn a profit for the fund's share-holders. Many mutual funds specialize in owning a particular kind or group of securities. For example, some funds buy only stocks, whereas other funds limit their invest-ments to bonds; and some mutual funds buy only stocks issued in a particular country or in a particular region of the world. Likewise, some mutual funds invest only in tax-exempt bonds.

Mutual funds are nothing other than ready-made portfo-lios. Rather than investing in several different stocks or several different bonds, you need only invest in a mutual fund with an investment goal similar to your own. If you seek current income, you should select a mutual fund that invests in bonds or in stocks with high dividend payouts. If your goals are more in tune with long-term growth, you should consider a mutual fund that buys stocks with good growth potential. There is nothing wrong with owning two mutual funds with different goals. For example, you may decide to invest part of your money in a fund that seeks long-term growth and the remainder of your money in a fund that seeks current income.

Mutual fund shares are not traded in the same manner as other securities. They are purchased directly from the fund's sponsor, who also redeems shares of the fund. The shares of some mutual funds are sold only through authorized sales-people, whereas other funds sell their shares directly to individual investors.

Be flexible in the brand you purchase. The more brands of a particular item you find acceptable, the more likely you are able to buy the item on sale.

Expenses are involved in buying and owning mutual funds. All mutual funds levy an annual management fee that ranges from .3 to 1.5 percent of the assets managed. Many funds also levy a sales fee when shares are purchased, or a redemption fee when shares are redeemed. All relevant fees are clearly spelled out in a document called a *prospectus*. You should carefully investigate these fees before investing in a mutual fund.

Life insurance

Life insurance is frequently sold as an investment vehicle that accumulates savings as well as pays death benefits. A life insurance policy builds savings when you pay premiums that exceed the cost of providing your death benefits. Most life insurance policies that incorporate savings require an annual premium payment that remains constant for the life of the policy or for a limited period specified in the policy. For example, you might purchase a $30,000 policy on which you must pay fixed annual premiums for twenty years. After twenty years, no further premiums are required even though the insurance remains in force. A policy with a limited number of payments can be offered only by charging premiums that are significantly higher than the cost of insuring you during the early years of the policy.

Life insurance offers you the benefit of being able to accumulate savings while deferring taxes on the accumulation. You are required to pay taxes only when you finally draw on the funds, and even then you will be taxed only on the difference between the amount you take out and the total of the premiums you paid over the life of the policy.

One problem with using life insurance as an investment

vehicle is the fees, which can be quite high. Cost is especially high when you buy a life insurance policy as an investment when you really don't need the insurance. Life insurance should be considered as an investment only if you plan to stash away the funds for a long time.

Annuities

Annuities are another investment product sold by insurance companies. An annuity is a stream of equal periodic payments. For example, you might purchase an annuity that pays you $600 per month for life beginning at age sixty-five. There are many flavors of annuities: Some annuities are guaranteed for a person's lifetime, some annuities make payments for a stipulated number of years, and some pay for life with a guaranteed number of payments.

Annuities can be purchased with a single payment or with a series of payments. Perhaps you inherit a large amount of money when you are in your thirties and become concerned that you will squander the funds away through bad investments and excessive consumption. You can use a portion or all of the funds to purchase an annuity that will begin making payments to you at whatever date you specify. Your funds will grow on a tax-deferred basis during the time between when you purchase the annuity and when you begin to draw payments.

A more common method of purchasing an annuity involves making annual or monthly payments to an insurance company for many years, at the end of which time you begin to draw on the annuity. For example, you may pay $100 per month during your working years in order to have a lifetime income that will begin at your retirement.

Annuities are generally used to provide individuals with supplemental sources of retirement income. Like life insurance, annuities often involve fairly large up-front costs and are not appropriate investments for individuals who are likely to need the funds in a matter of several years.

Tangible assets

Tangible investment assets—items of a physical nature—can provide protection against some of the risks encountered by someone who owns financial assets. Tangible assets include a house, rental property, jewelry, precious metals, a stamp collection, art, antiques, or even a baseball-card collection (if only I had my 1953 Topps set back!).

Because most tangible assets do not provide any periodic income payments (rental real estate is an exception), investors acquire these investments in order to profit from increases in value. Tangible assets tend to increase in value most when inflation is depleting the real values of financial assets. On the other hand, tangible assets may provide little or no return during periods of stable consumer prices.

Tangible assets are often difficult to dispose of compared to financial assets, which have active secondary markets. As a result, tangible assets are more appropriate to acquire when a lengthy holding period is expected. The fees and markups on most tangible assets are too large to attempt to earn a reasonable return from a short holding period.

Don't assume something is better just because it costs more. Cost is not always a good indicator of value. Try a less expensive substitute and compare it with your usual brand. If you can't detect a difference in quality, choose the lower-priced item.

Glossary

annuity   A series of periodic payments received for a stipulated period of time or for a lifetime.

asset   Something of value. Assets are generally measured in terms of their current fair market value.

balanced budget   A budget in which income for the budget period equals expenditures.

balance sheet   A financial statement that list assets, liabilities, and the net worth at a particular point in time.

bond   A long-term debt security. Most bonds pay fixed semiannual interest to a prescribed maturity date, at which time the face amount of the bond is repaid to the bondholder.

budgeting   A system of financial planning and control that involves careful monitoring of income and expenses.

cash budget   A system of financial planning in which only cash expenditures and cash income items are considered.

cash value   The accumulation of savings in a life insurance policy. A policy's cash value can be used as a source of loan collateral.

cash value life insurance   Life insurance that includes savings.

common stock   Units of ownership in a business enterprise.

Consumer Price Index (CPI)   A relative measure of prices for goods and services purchased by individuals and families compared to a base year.

credit bureau A private organization that collects and maintains credit information about individual borrowers.

creditor A person or institution to whom money is owed.

credit rating A rating designed to measure a borrower's ability to repay debt.

credit statement A financial statement of the charges, finance charges, and payments on a credit account.

credit union A financial institution formed to serve members who have some common bond.

debt An amount owed to a creditor.

debt limit The maximum amount a loan applicant may borrow.

deficit The amount by which spending exceeds income. A deficit may be offset by borrowing funds or dipping into savings.

depreciation Loss in value of an asset as time passes.

dividend A portion of the profits a company distributes to its stockholders. Most companies pay quarterly dividends.

earned income Income from employment.

effective rate of interest The rate of interest actually earned on savings or charged on a loan.

equity Ownership interest in an asset or group of assets. Your equity in a house is equal to its market value less any outstanding amount owed on the mortgage.

estate   Wealth accumulated over a lifetime.

estate tax   A tax on an estate that is imposed before making any distribution to heirs.

estimated taxes   Taxes due on income not subject to withholding. Estimated taxes are supposed to be paid quarterly.

expenditure   Money spent on a good or service.

fair market value   The price a willing buyer would currently pay to purchase an item.

financial statement   A compilation of selected financial data. An income statement and balance sheet are two examples of financial statements.

fixed expense   An outlay that generally remains the same from one installment period to the next. Mortgage payments, rent, and insurance premiums are examples of fixed expenses.

fixed income   Income that remains the same from one period to the next. Bonds, pensions, and annuities are generally sources of fixed income.

flexible expense   An outlay that varies in amount from one period to the next. Individuals and families generally have considerable control over flexible expenses. Also called a *variable expense*.

gross pay   Income earned before employer deductions for taxes, social security, insurance, and so forth.

inflation   A decline in the purchasing power of money as time passes.

installment credit   Consumer credit in which the borrower is required to make equal periodic payments to the creditor.

intestate   Pertaining to an individual who has died without leaving a valid will.

IRA   Individual Retirement Account—a custodial retirement account in which an individual may set aside earned income on a tax-deferred basis.

liability   An amount owed.

liquidity   How easily an asset can be converted to a known amount of cash.

marginal tax rate   The rate of taxation on each extra dollar of taxable income. The marginal tax rate should be used in making personal economic decisions.

money market deposit account   A type of savings account offered by depository institutions in which funds are invested in short-term marketable securities. The account generally includes certain restrictions on required balances and checkwriting but pays a higher return than conventional savings accounts.

money market mutual fund   A mutual fund that pools investors' funds in short-term marketable securities.

mutual fund   An investment company that pools investors' funds and invests them in accordance with stated goals. Dividends, interest, and capital gains are passed through to shareholders, who are responsible for paying taxes on income received. Mutual funds stand ready to redeem their outstanding shares for cash.

net pay   Earned income after employer deductions for taxes, social security, insurance, and so forth.

net worth   Available cash plus assets owned free and clear of debt. Net worth is calculated by deducting liabilities from cash on hand and the current market value of assets.

overwithholding   The amount an employer withholds from an employee's pay beyond what is needed to meet the employee's tax liability.

portfolio   A collection of investment assets.

prime rate   The short-term interest rate charged by commercial banks on loans to their best customers.

principal   The amount still owed on a loan or the amount invested in a certificate of deposit or bond.

risk   Uncertainty of a financial outcome.

secured loan   A loan on which repayment is guaranteed by specific assets.

surplus   The amount by which income exceeds spending. A surplus adds to savings.

taxable income   The amount of income subject to taxation.

tax liability   Tax owed to a government authority.

tax-sheltered retirement plan   An IRS-approved plan that qualifies for special tax advantages that serve to increase retirement benefits. An IRA is an example of a tax-sheltered retirement plan.

term life insurance   Life insurance that pays benefits only upon the insured's death. No savings are accumulated.

Treasury securities   Debt obligations of the U.S. government.

unearned income   Money received from a source other than employment. Interest and dividends are examples of unearned income.

variable expense   See *flexible expense.*

variable-rate loan   A loan on which the interest rate charged by the creditor is subject to change at periodic intervals according to some specified index.

yield   The return earned on an investment expressed as a percentage of the amount invested or the current market value. Yield is generally stated on an annual basis.

Index

Accrued basis, as used
by business, 11
Amortized loan, 56
Annuities, investing in,
138
Assets, 44
bonds, value of, 52
car, value of, 48, 49,
51
certificates of deposit
(CDs), value of, 48,
53
checking accounts,
value of, 53
collectibles, value of,
52
collecting information
about your, 49–55
current, 45
home, value of, 48,
49, 50
jewelry, value of, 49,
52
life insurance, value
of, 53–54
mutual funds, value
of, 53
retirement plans/
accounts, value of,
54–55
savings accounts,
value of, 48, 53
securities, value of,
48, 52
stocks, value of, 52

Balance sheet
assets, 45–55

liabilities, 45–49,
55–58, 79–80
net worth, 46, 58–59
personal versus busi-
ness, 44–49
spreadsheet example
for constructing a,
96–100
what it is, 43–44
Bank accounts
checking, 21, 53,
69–73, 125–26
interest income from,
64–65
money market de-
posit, 126–28
savings, 48, 53
Bonds
asset value of, 52
investing in, 122, 124,
130–31, 133–34
Budgeting
building a record of
expenses, 67–75
combining forecasts,
81–84
debt payments, incor-
porating, 79–80
discrepancies in, 89–92
evaluating forecasts,
84–92
family involvement in,
22–24
forecasts of expenses,
10–11, 61, 67–76
forecasts of income,
10–11, 61–67
frame of mind and, 15

goals, financial, 8–9,
23, 25–42
how to start, 13–24
information you will
need for, 20–21
intelligent consumer
and, 7
items you will need
for, 16–19
as an ongoing project,
92–93
personal versus busi-
ness, 10–12
revisions, 63, 80
selecting a budgeting
period, 62
spreadsheet programs
and, 89–111
summary sheet,
spreadsheet
example for con-
structing, 111–14
time needed for, 14
what it can do, 6–9
what it is, 1–2
who will benefit from,
2–3
who will not benefit
from, 5–6
Business, investing in a
private, 123, 130

Calculator, 19
Car insurance
collision and compre-
hensive coverage,
canceling, 86
Cars

Index

paycheck stub, 20
relationship between
  expenses and, 6–7
rental property, 64
retirement plan/
  account, 64
social security in-
  come, 64
spreadsheet example
  for recording,
  94–98
tax return, federal in-
  come, 20, 64
Inflation, goals and,
  29–33, 125
Insurance
  buying only what you
    need, 85
  car, 86
  life, 53–54
  shopping for, 85
Intelligent consumer,
    the
  budgeting and, 7
  coupons, 52
  credit card balances,
    paying off, 3, 120
  credit cards, shop-
    ping, 7
  insurance shopping
    tips, 85
  investment shopping
    tips, 12, 14, 20, 89,
    97, 127
  newspapers, 51, 52
  pressure, avoiding
    buying under, 53
  quantities, buying
    large, 6
  restaurant meals ver-
    sus eating at home,

54, 64
sales/special prices,
  10, 62, 136
supermarket shopping
  tips, 6, 33, 52, 62,
  71, 74
unit pricing, 33
Interest income, 64–67

Jewelry, asset value of,
  49, 52

Ledger pad, 16–18,
  74–75
Liabilities, 45, 47
  car loans, 46, 56–57
  collecting information
    about your, 55–58
  credit card debt, 3,
    21, 46, 57–58, 124
  incorporating debt
    payments into your
    budget, 79–80
  mortgage loans, 46,
    49, 56
  personal loans, 58
Life insurance
  asset value of, 53–54
  investing in, 137–38
  shopping for, 85
Lotus 1-2-3 (spread-
  sheet program), 95
  budgeting example
    using, 96–114

Maintenance, car, 11,
  77
Memo pads, 18
Money market deposit
  accounts, investing
  in, 126–28

Money market funds,
  investing in,
  128–29
Mortgage loans, 46,
  49, 56
Mutual funds
  asset value of, 53
  investing in, 122, 127,
    130, 135–37

Net worth, 46, 59–60
Newspapers, 51–52
Notebooks, 18, 71–73,
  84–86

Opportunity cost, 3

Paycheck stub, 20
Pencils, 16
Personal loans, 58–59
Personal versus business
  balance sheet,
  44–49
Personal versus business
  budgeting, 10–12
Pressure, avoiding buy-
  ing under, 53

Quantities, buying
  large, 6
Quattro Pro (spread-
  sheet program), 96

Rental property
  income from, 64
  investing in, 130, 139
Restaurant meals, eat-
  ing at home versus,
  54, 64
Retirement plans/
  accounts
  asset value of, 54–55

- 149 -

About the Author

David L. Scott is Professor of Accounting and Finance at Valdosta State University, Valdosta, Georgia. Professor Scott was born in Rushville, Indiana, and received degrees from Purdue University and Florida State University before earning a PhD in economics at the University of Arkansas at Fayetteville.

Dr. Scott teaches financial management and investments and has offered workshops in personal investing and personal budgeting. He has written twenty-six books, including *Wall Street Words* for Houghton Mifflin, *How Wall Street Works* for Irwin Professional Publishing, and seven other titles in the Money Smarts series. He and his wife, Kay, are the authors of the two-volume *Guide to the National Park Areas* published by The Globe Pequot Press. The two writers travel around the country during the summers in their fourth Volkswagen camper.